Best Wishes

McCLEAN DESIGN

McCLEAN DESIGN: CREATING THE CONTEMPORARY HOUSE

PHILIP JODIDIO

New York · Paris · London · Milan

- 6 **FOREWORD** BY VALERIE MULVIN AND NIALL McCULLOUGH
- 8 **PREFACE** BY PAUL McCLEAN
- 10 **THE WHOLE IDEA: RESIDENTIAL ARCHITECTURE** BY PHILIP JODIDIO

24 **VIA MAJORCA** 2008	120 **DOHENY** 2016
32 **BLUE JAY WAY** 2008/2017	128 **HILLCREST** 2016
44 **SARBONNE** 2011	138 **MARCHEETA** 2016
54 **ORIOLE DRIVE** 2012	148 **HILLCREST II** 2016
64 **ORIOLE WAY** 2012	158 **BLUE JAY WAY III** 2017
74 **SAN VICENTE** 2013	168 **DEVLIN** 2017
86 **CARLA RIDGE** 2014	180 **ROBIN** 2018
96 **TEMPLE HILLS** 2014	192 **SUNRIDGE** 2018
104 **TANAGER III** 2014	202 **BEL AIR** 2018
112 **WILLIAMS** 2015	214 **CARLA LANE** 2018
	224 **SKYLARK** 2018

236 APPENDIX

FOREWORD
BY VALERIE MULVIN AND NIALL McCULLOUGH

Trinity Long Room Hub, by McCullough Mulvin Architects, Humanities Research Building, Trinity College, Dublin, Ireland, 2010.

I've a strong memory of Paul McClean and two models he was working on almost thirty years ago in Dublin—artists' studios in Temple Bar and an extension to the Abbey Theatre. Paul was a brilliant model maker and models were (and still are) essential to our design process, so many hours were spent discussing and dissecting them, with Paul listening carefully, then obsessively working and reworking the pieces, meticulously counterpointing new forms against existing ones with clarity and judgment until they got across exactly the point of each scheme. Architectural education at that time in Ireland—and our own work—was strongly influenced by the European-focused teachings of Aldo Rossi, texts such as Kenneth Frampton's "Towards a Critical Regionalism: Six Points for an Architecture of Resistance," and the canonical modernism of Le Corbusier, Ludwig Mies van der Rohe, Louis Kahn, and Alvar Aalto. Their backbone of structure, light, and materials permeated all the schemes we were working on—at that time a number of city projects that reimagined urban quarters and threw focus back on living in the city. It was urban dentistry in rundown areas of town, where vitality was underpinned by an eclectic mix of uses—secondhand bookshops, vintage clothes, artists studios, music venues—all thriving on short-term rents and the threat of imminent demolition. Paul's models became part of the arsenal of persuasion used to encourage developers to re-inhabit existing urban fabric and build on derelict sites. One project was finally built, one not, but those models—one of which still exists in the archive—translated our thinking into three-dimensional form with spirit and dexterity.

Exchanging the changeable skies of Dublin for the solid blue ones of Southern California, and working with a new palette of color, landscape, and materials, Paul—like many Irish emigrants before him full of ideas, vision, and energy—has carved out a remarkable life in a new country. He has created a strong and architectonic body of work that he modestly describes as "residential modernism." It perhaps draws from the modernist canon of the Case Study Houses of the 1950s with their sense of private and privileged retreat from the world, hovering above—and somehow fueled by—the city below. Those houses, captured in the beautiful photography of Julius Shulman, depict the rarefied world of movie stars, swimming pools, tropical plants, and desert air, where life is frozen in the interrupted drama of leisure, where spaces exist not just to live in, but as ideal worlds within which to dream, suspended above the city, portrayed as an unfeeling grid stretching to the horizon or to the ocean.

Paul's houses for the twenty-first century inhabit territory similar to that of the Case Study Houses, in the dream world of a Southern Californian life in the hills above the grid of the city. They are buildings that create an ultimate retreat from the world where their owners can live an expansive life with family and friends, screened from the glare of publicity.

When building within tightly controlled zones of what is probably the most rarefied real estate in the world, the architectural game requires skillfully striking a balance between creating totally private space, screening views of adjoining houses, and framing a view. Under multiple constraints, the houses manage to create a sense of calm monumentality, generated by a strong, regular beat of structure and a clear sequence of spaces. Essential to this in almost all cases is a meticulously constructed architectural promenade from screened motor court entrance, across or along the plan and section, to an edited view to the horizon from main living spaces. This is achieved via a crafted sequence that rotates you at significant moments to exploit the dimensions of the site, extending spatial drama and drawing in nature at every possible point. The common thread across these precisely modulated sequences is the use of water, whether as a threshold element crossed by a bridge; an introductory wall of spilling water reducing background noise; or still reflective pools offering calm in front of a huge view.

Planimetrically, there is great skill in creating rectilinear geometries across these irregular plot shapes, and the resultant edge conditions sometimes allow another geometry to come into play. Hence, circles resolve odd corners, create generous arrival spaces, and make platforms around which to gather communal activity, and helical stairs dramatically float you from floor to floor.

In section, a sandwich of horizontal planes, in the tradition of twentieth-century International Style modernism, creates intimacy for each floor level while delivering large, interconnected spaces for life to flow. These comparatively compressed floor-to-ceiling heights are released by the remarkable views achieved with carefully controlled placement of major rooms. Usually one entire wall of a living space is framed out to dramatic views of landscape and ocean—the infinite, the sky and sea, one dimension always open and free. The selection of these curated viewing points achieves for each house something unique and individually true about each site, and the lateral extension across stepped terraces—requiring great architectonic skill—creates a receding series of planes that expand the sense of spatial complexity. In a similar way, internal staircases and solid planes generate areas of dynamic movement through the section, counterpointing the calm of living spaces with dynamic views.

Palettes of materials are precious and fine throughout and include classic marbles and figured stone and timber. Planes of glass offer views or create reflections that dissolve boundaries; floor plates of the same material link spaces and float out toward the horizon, extending spatial enjoyment. These materials are revealed through the joyous play of light on their surfaces, interrupted by flashes of nature that relax the eye and open to the infinite.

These are houses where space itself and the materials that define its boundaries are finely crafted and thoroughly understood as the background to the Southern California dream.

Valerie Mulvin and Niall McCullough are the principals of McCullough Mulvin Architects in Dublin.

PREFACE
BY PAUL McCLEAN

As I woke up on a Greyhound bus after a long journey sometime in October of 1990, my first impression of California was the occasional glimpse of ghostly oak-clad hills through the early morning gray before the Bay Bridge loomed out of the mist. A little while later as I walked away from the bus station, the sky was revealed to be an intense blue as watery fog receded across the bay beyond the Ferry Building at the end of Market Street. I moved to Southern California a few years later and the constant play between water and light has continued to inspire me ever since. This place of amazing natural beauty has been very good to me, and I have met many wonderful people here who have allowed McClean Design to help build their dreams on ground that is inclined to move once in a while.

California has always been a place where people come from somewhere else to start over, hoping for a different life. From the gold rush, through the birth of Hollywood, to the orange groves that once enveloped the southland. The history of Los Angeles cannot be separated from that of the film industry, run by people who created celluloid dreams by day and went home to architectural fantasies at night—fantasies designed by architects also in search of a place that would allow them to explore and be creative in new ways. They saw this new city in the making as a blank slate, and over the course of a century created an unparalleled catalogue of residential architecture that has inspired people across the globe and, in particular, a young lad growing up in suburban Dublin.

The city of Los Angeles continues to grow, pushing up against the natural boundaries of the mountains and the ocean, densifying at its core while continuing to expand ever outward. It is within this vast urban sprawl that we find ourselves designing most of our projects, drawing inspiration from a legacy of modern homes that connect to nature in ways that would often be impossible in traditional cities. The clear desert light and a warm climate that is nearly always benign help us to dissolve boundaries between indoor

Original sketch from the first project designed by Paul McClean after establishing McClean Design: a canyon house in Laguna Beach, California, 2002.

A house currently under construction at Lake Folsom in Northern California.

and outdoor space and create connections to the landscape beyond. The landscape continues to be our primary source of inspiration no matter where we are working, and we try to create houses that connect seamlessly with both their immediate surroundings and their environs.

Houses are currently the focus of our practice and I hope they will continue to be. They are often the most challenging of projects; typically, a client builds a custom home only once, and doing so is usually the most expensive undertaking someone embarks upon in a lifetime. It requires careful balancing of many requirements and figuring out how best to organize the required program, the complexities of the site, climate, and neighborhood, as well as taking into account the owner's personal preferences, beliefs, and eccentricities. There are many types of buildings, but home is a fundamental concept that everyone can appreciate and understand. I am still surprised by the amazing sites we are offered to build upon, their views of the mountains, the city, and the ocean, how adjacent locations can be so different and the dynamism that can produce. In the last few years we have started to work in different locations and climates across North America and beyond. Much translates, but each new environment presents different challenges and creates different responses that help us to expand our thinking.

Our intent in designing a home is to get beyond what is programmatically required and into something that enriches the lives of its inhabitants while helping them connect to the natural world around them. Creating a sense of calm and privacy seems ever more important in the modern world, which is so full of noise and distraction. Space seems to have become the most important of luxuries today. We hope our projects can help provide some respite for their users, a place to recharge and contemplate nature and the world around them. We try to create spaces that are uplifting but do not dominate, strong enough to engage with the site and the landscape, but quiet enough not to get in the way of everyday life.

We are so fortunate in what we do; having work that you are passionate about is one of the greatest gifts. Speaking of thanks, I could not continue without expressing deep gratitude for all the clients who have taken a chance with us over the years; we have all been on this journey together. A special thanks to the McKillen family, Nile Niami, and Cody Leibel, with whom we have worked on multiple projects for many years now, and to my wife and family for all their continuous encouragement and support. In our office we work as a close-knit team and everyone deserves equal credit for the work in this volume. Thanks to all of you. I never imagined this place of dreams would allow me to fulfill so many of my own.

THE WHOLE IDEA: RESIDENTIAL ARCHITECTURE

A 1903 Pacific Heights mansion renovation in San Francisco that involved a complete interior remodel as well as new rooftop pool and basement garage, 2015.

Capital of the entertainment industry, sprawling with its larger metropolitan area over 30,000 square miles, Los Angeles is the paradise of the automobile, where freeways define all movement. The dreams fabricated in Hollywood and Disneyland exist side by side with the complex realities of a contemporary American city, exemplifying the contrasts that make up the reality of the second largest city in the United States. Blessed by nature in many ways, yet sitting astride the San Andreas fault, Los Angeles is a city where anything goes, a place where everything can change unexpectedly, and nothing seems permanent With average temperatures that range from 55°F in January to 72°F in August, Los Angeles has one of the most temperate climates anywhere, a fact that is conducive to outdoor living, to open houses and swimming pools, and surely to good humor. Its hills and beaches overlook city and ocean, meaning that spectacular views are the norm rather than the exception.

Reinventing the Private House

Southern California has indeed long been known for its remarkable private houses, designed by some of the most famous architects of the twentieth and twenty-first centuries. The image of California as the new American paradise most probably dates from the time of the rate wars between the Santa Fe and Southern Pacific railroads. A flood of new arrivals in the state after 1887 included a number of talented architects from the East who began, very early on, to create exceptional private homes. Amongst them were Charles and Henry Greene, who had been working in Boston before they established their practice, Greene & Greene, in Pasadena in 1894. Although they experimented with a number of styles, they are best known for works such as the Gamble House (Pasadena, 1908), which was inspired by the English Arts and Crafts movement, by the elaborate framing and joinery of Japanese architecture, and certainly by the favorable climate of Southern California. Their insistence on high standards of craftsmanship was blended with a pragmatic acceptance of mechanical production, and as such they had a strong influence on the evolution of the concept of the specifically Californian house.

Another arrival before the turn of the century was Irving Gill, who was born in Tully, New York. Gill worked with the firm of Adler and Sullivan in Chicago under Frank Lloyd Wright before settling in San Diego in 1893. Gill modified the Mission style in a way that foreshadowed the clean lines of modernism, and also dared to use concrete extensively in the 1890s. He favored flat roofs without eaves and mainly white exterior and interior walls, as well as cubic or rectangular massing. Gill's Horatio West Court (Santa Monica, 1919) had a direct influence on the work of Richard Neutra, who photographed and published the project in his book *Amerika: Neues Bauen in der Welt* (1930). The critic Aaron Betsky wrote of Gill, "He developed an architecture of abstract white forms that seem both thoroughly modern and rooted to the place."[1]

More than anyone else early in the twentieth century, Frank Lloyd Wright gave impetus to Southern California's interest in contemporary architecture. Between 1917 and 1925, he designed more than forty projects for the region and built seven houses there. Wright rejected the Mission style in favor of a "local" influence that he found more significant—that of the Mayans. Born in Vienna in 1887, Rudolph Schindler came to the United States in 1914 and became an assistant to Wright. Schindler remained in Southern California, where, together with his compatriot and friend Richard Neutra, he played a central role in the acceptance of modern architecture. Schindler's own residence (Schindler-Chase House, West Hollywood, 1922) employs a Japanese concept of indoor/outdoor space that is particularly well-adapted to the local climate, combined with a strong sense of rectilinear modernity.

Influenced by Adolf Loos, Neutra worked in the early 1920s for Erich Mendelsohn, architect of the Einstein Tower (Potsdam, 1919–21), before coming to the United States in 1923, and working briefly for Wright in 1924. He and Schindler participated unsuccessfully in the 1926–27 Palace of the League of Nations competition, but it was their meeting with Philip and Leah Lovell that was to form their reputations. In the mid-1920s, Schindler built three vacation houses for the Lovells, the most famous of which is the Lovell Beach House (Newport Beach, 1922–26). Lifted up on ferro-concrete piers for reasons of privacy as well as to enhance the view from the balconies, this residence is the prototypical California beach house. Neutra and Schindler had a falling out over the next commission awarded by the Lovells, but Neutra's Lovell Health House (Griffith Park, 1929) was the first steel-framed house conceived in the International Style in the United States.

In 1943, John Entenza, editor of the magazine *Arts & Architecture*, organized a competition under the title "Designs for Post-War Living." Foreseeing a need for large-scale housing construction, Entenza and Charles Eames wrote an essay in an issue of the magazine published in 1944 calling for the conversion of wartime industrial technologies in the service of home building. The Case Study House Program was announced in the January 1945 issue of *Arts & Architecture*. Between that time and 1966, a total of thirty-four designs, intended as prototypical models of modern architecture for Southern California, were published in the magazine, and twenty-three were actually built. Amongst the eight original participants in the program were Eames, Eero Saarinen, and Neutra; they were joined later by others, such as Craig Ellwood and Pierre Koenig.

The Whole Idea

John Lautner, who was trained by Wright and had a career that spanned fifty-five years up to his death in 1994, is another example of the type of original architect this environment has encouraged. Lautner was known for his ability to make use of the topography and natural settings of Los Angeles to the best advantage. He created such iconic structures as the Chemosphere House on Torreyson Drive (1960) with its nearly 360-degree view of the city and the Sheats-Goldstein Residence (Beverly Crest, Los Angeles, 1963), for which he designed not only the house, but the interiors, windows, lighting, rugs, furniture, and operable features. The living room was originally completely open to the terrace, protected by only a curtain of forced air. Of his apprenticeship in the 1930s with Wright, Lautner later said, "Mr. Wright was around all the time pointing out things that contributed to the beauty of the space, or the building, or the function of the kitchen, or the dining room, or what-have-you. And also the details of construction: how a certain way of detailing, which he would call grammar, contributed to the whole idea, the whole, the total expression. And then he kept accenting the idea that there wasn't any real architecture unless you had a whole idea, so… I really learned that you have to have a major total idea or it's nothing, you know; it's just an assembly. What most people do is an assembly of clichés or façades or what-have-you."[2] From Wright to Lautner and beyond, there is a filiation in the creation of the modern Southern California house that underlies much of what is done even today. Wright, Neutra, Lautner, and those who have followed reinvented the modern house in the particular circumstances of the California climate, but with an influence that has been international.

Break with the Dictum

More recently, residential architecture in Los Angeles has been marked by the presence of figures as diverse as Frank Gehry, Richard Meier, and Tadao Ando. Based in Los Angeles, Gehry made his early reputation with a number of private homes, including his own house on 22nd Street in Santa Monica. Gehry's sense of architecture as sculptural form reached its height with the Schnabel Residence (Brentwood, 1989). Copper, lead-coated copper panels, and stucco cover a symphony of shapes that make up this remarkable house, part of which floats on a small artificial pond. Far removed in its abrupt angles and compositional complexity from the radical simplicity sought in many of the Case Study Houses, the Schnabel Residence represents a high point of what a 1988 exhibition organized by Philip Johnson and Mark Wigley at the Museum of Modern Art in New York called "Deconstructivist Architecture." More than a superficial decorative scheme, the Schnabel Residence represents an effort to break with the Miesian dictum that "Form follows function."

In the past few years, the influx of foreign buyers and the newly-minted wealthy from the tech and entertainment industries has driven the property market in Los Angeles and created demand for luxury homes that are often conceived with a sense of architectural style,[3] or in any case with an eye to selecting a well-known architect. Richard Meier (Ackerberg House, 1994; Malibu Beach House, 2006) and Tadao Ando (House in Malibu III, 2012) have built on privileged sites on the beach, while others, like Thom Mayne of Morphosis, have created their own homes in the city (Sixth Street House, 1987; Cheviot Hills House, 2017). In their own ways, each of these architects has applied a determined style to his own version of the Southern California house, surely updating the accepted themes and forms that originated with Schindler, Neutra, and the Case Study Houses. Views, designs that link interior and exterior, and, indeed, an overall sense of continuity and quality nonetheless are guiding elements even in the recent homes in Los Angeles designed by celebrated architects.

Beach house on Seacliff Drive in Laguna Beach, California, 2013.

From Dublin to Orange

Born in 1968, Paul McClean grew up in Dublin. He attended the Dublin Institute of Technology architectural program and graduated with honors in architecture in 1994 from the University of Dublin. During his time at the university, he travelled extensively and worked for architectural practices in Dublin, London, and Sydney. Subsequent to his third year of studies, he spent a year in Australia, working in the office of Dennis Rourke Architects on residential projects. After his fourth year, McClean worked for a year with McCullough Mulvin Architects in Dublin on museums and art galleries. In retrospect, McClean does maintain that Ireland has a continuing importance for his work. "I think it continues to influence me in subtle ways," he says. "Despite the scale of the Los Angeles projects, it brings a dose of realism to my thinking and I feel that helps to keep the projects rational. I was heavily influenced by the sense of proportion that can be found in Georgian Dublin and that still comes through in our work, I think, in the relationships between solid and void, for example."[4]

In 1994, Paul McClean followed in the footsteps of many talented architects who went west. He moved to California and began to work in Laguna Beach at first with Accolade Interiors on healthcare projects and then with Horst Architects on houses in the area. Even before coming to California, McClean was looking to the influence of some of its noted architects, often those who were known for their work on private houses. He explains, "First I found Frank Lloyd Wright as a kid. As I grew into architecture and started studying it and developed a passion for homes, Richard Neutra stood out the most in my mind. I always liked the clean lines that he worked with. I also admired Craig Ellwood from the Case Studies period. I like the work of John Lautner, but it is slightly different from the direction that I took."

Achieving Simplicity

Unlike some architects who are reluctant to speak about the influences that have formed their creativity, Paul McClean is forthright about this issue. "I love Richard Meier's work and he has always been a huge influence on me," he says. "I often look at his plans and elevations when I am starting a project. The way he puts spaces together is really wonderful. It is a different direction from what I do, but it is inspirational to me." Meier's work is, of course, based on strict grids and repetitive use of white materials in most cases. These grids are willfully expressed throughout his houses, with precise alignments and careful detailing being the hallmarks of a style that is one of the most recognizable in contemporary architecture. McClean also has a palette of modern forms that he calls upon, but he does not make such visible use of rectilinear grids as his older New York colleague. Though McClean clearly favors clarity in design, he also has found interest in the background of some of his older colleagues. Amongst English architects, for example, he says, "Norman Foster is the one I gravitate to—it is about simplicity and clean lines. The hardest thing to achieve is that simplicity. I was also inspired by Norman Foster's life history. I grew up in a very modest background. We lived in a small house and I had no contact with anyone in the architectural world. It all came later. He grew up with a similar background." Current favorites of McClean on the West Coast include the firm Aidlin Darling Design in the Bay Area and Olson Kundig, based in Seattle.

Centered in Los Angeles

Paul McClean founded his firm McClean Design in Orange, California in 2000, when he built a residence in the Canyon Acres area of Laguna Beach. During its first five years, the office worked on coastal houses in Laguna Beach and Newport Beach, both south of Los Angeles. Its first Hollywood Hills project, on Blue Jay Way, started up in 2005. The publicity surrounding this project led to the firm receiving more commissions in Los Angeles, and by 2013, the majority of its work was in Los Angeles, as opposed to Orange County.

McClean first met the developer Nile Niami in 2010 and started a fruitful collaboration that continues today. Niami noticed the original Blue Jay Way house and contacted McClean about working on a speculative project in the same neighborhood. A native Angeleno, Nile Niami began his career as a movie producer, using skills that he continued to hone to create and stage luxury lifestyle homes in an almost cinematic way. Prior to 2010, Niami was already building homes, but he correctly surmised that despite the recession there would soon be a market for luxury contemporary homes in the prime districts of Los Angeles. The city was just beginning to attract wealthy buyers from out of state and abroad for potential second or third homes. McClean remembers how tenacious Niami was in trying to get their first project up and running. Almost a year went by before he could secure financing for their house on Tanager Way. During that design and build process, McClean introduced Niami to his friend and mentor Patrick "Paddy" McKillen, whose son Dean had just arrived in California. Niami went on to collaborate with the McKillens on a Beverly Hills project and the Oriole Drive house before continuing to develop homes independently.

Pacific Palisades, Los Angeles. This three-level Casale residence was completed in 2016.

Niami is credited by many in the real estate market with singlehandedly kick-starting a new luxury market that has blossomed across the west side of Los Angeles and attracts a growing international clientele. His unique signature style can be seen in several of the homes in this volume and will be most apparent in what might be said to be the ultimate Los Angeles house, known as "The One," designed by McClean and due to be completed as this book goes to press. The property has twenty bedrooms—the largest of which is a 5,500-square-foot master suite—and multiple elevators and swimming pools, making it one of the most spectacular homes ever created in Los Angeles. The home is being finished to Niami's exacting standards with the intention to create an unrivaled "lifestyle experience" with amenities usually found only in luxury resorts and hotels.

From a Sketch to a Home

McClean Design's client base has continued to expand over the last ten years. Today, the firm employs ten additional architects and supporting staff under the leadership of Paul McClean and it continues to concentrate on "high-end residential design." Its projects remain a mixture of homes for individual clients and houses for sale built in collaboration with developers such as Niami and McKillen. Although the architect wishes not to enlarge the office substantially in order to maintain "a highly personal approach," McClean Design has begun to work in states other than California, including Hawaii, and in Canada.

The work methods of McClean Design are quite straightforward. Although Paul McClean does sketches to clarify his ideas, his firm then takes projects forward using computer assisted design tools. "Generally I start by assigning someone as project manager and have them help me figure out the site and code parameters, as well as attend client meetings where we develop the program in conjunction with the client," he explains. "Once we have that initial information I sit down with pen and paper and try and work the information into an initial concept. This is usually in the form of sketches and rough floor plans. Once I feel I have developed a good starting point, I regroup with the project manager and we develop a model in SketchUp, which is often shared within the office and manipulated until it starts to resemble the initial concept. Once we are happy with it, we meet with the client and share presentation-level drawings, and then we go on to develop the design further. It may take several rounds before the design works well enough with their program—sometimes it goes much faster, though. Once both we and the client are satisfied with the model and we are sure it can receive planning approval, it is converted using CAD software. CAD construction documents are required now and we are moving into three-dimensional documents, which I think will eventually significantly improve productivity, leaving more time for design and discussion." McClean Design has been fortunate enough to grow in good part on the basis of favorable word-of-mouth, but it has recently noted an upswing in new commissions based on social media, particularly for projects at a distance from Los Angeles.

Clean Lines and Falling Water

The houses of McClean Design are clearly conceived in direct response to sites and client programs. They do share a sense of crisp modernity, and the "clean lines" that the architect cites with reference to Richard Meier and Norman Foster, and a certain number of other features as well. Since most of the houses are located in Southern California, which has a dry, subtropical climate, the architect has frequently found it useful to introduce water elements in his designs. The reasons for this are numerous and complex. Swimming pools are nearly ubiquitous in the region, as they provide relief and contrast to the warmth and dryness of the climate. In particular on sloped sites, McClean makes use of infinity pools. When extended in front of the house, this type of pool makes the connection between living spaces and the view more direct and at the same time reflects the sky. Another result of such designs is to shield a house from views of houses that may exist lower on the same slopes. In McClean Design houses, water from an infinity pool or water-covered walls also serve to connect one level of a house to the other and to augment the refracted light that reaches basement areas. McClean states, "Water has been used extensively in design for thousands of years in dry climates. As well as its obvious emotional draw, it can help with natural cooling and ventilation. Careful use of cross-ventilation will add moisture to the dry air around a pool and naturally condition the air, which can limit the need for air conditioning on moderately warm days." Many of the sites available in Southern California are sloped, and as a result the designs often work to connect spaces across gaps or intentional openings. McClean has found that bridges serve practical purposes in such cases, but also that they generate a "change in emotion" in residents and guests.

The Challenge of the Hillside

When McClean was doing his earliest residential work with Horst Architects, he found himself frequently working on hillside lots, and that continues to be the case today at his own firm. He says, "These sites pose specific access issues. How do you approach a house that is on a hillside? If there is downhill access, we take a lot of time trying to figure out how to avoid making people realize that they have a climb to get to the front door. We work with the topography and the views and try to make that journey eventful. If you look at a stairway that goes up two flights, it can appear to be intimidating. If you see half a flight of stairs and then a landing and a place to look at a view, then you turn around and you see a water feature a little bit further along, there is a way to manage that journey and make it more of an experience rather than something to be intimidated by." Progressively revealing what makes his work interesting, McClean also describes his approach to the ways in which light falls on a hillside, mainly on the outward side. "You are usually dealing with light that is coming only from one direction, which is not ideal," he says. "We like to try to get light from at least two directions. We have decided to move the houses as much as possible away from the slope, and that led us to create more courtyards and light wells. This was to bring light in and to keep the house away from problematic retaining walls."

This process is often complicated by the fact that the lots can be tight. Neighboring houses need to be "edited out" to enhance privacy, as the architect puts it. "We think a lot about editing," he says, "editing the experience of being in a room. Ideally you don't want to see anybody. You just want to see the distant view, and not be aware of any rooftops or any neighbors or potential sound issues from the street." Sound can be mitigated by water features, adjusted to the levels of street noise. McClean also makes careful use of trees and hedges to edit spaces so that the focus is on distant views. Appropriately enough in a city that is used to the movies, McClean sees the work he does as being similar to creating a set. "The houses can be oriented toward the most spectacular available view," he says. "In a way it is a little like doing stage sets. You try to positively manipulate the environment you have and to minimize the negative aspects. You also want to maximize the usable area on a property. On a hillside that is always tricky. Sometimes we project the building out to create a kind of precarious view. You feel that you are actually floating in that view. That is another relationship to theatricality that may exist."

Private houses designed by architects sometimes encounter problems with interiors that are done by other people in styles that may not be in keeping with the architectural

Entry courtyard of a Bel Air estate, the Cuesta House, Los Angeles, 2017.

intent. A glance at the houses designed and built by McClean since 2005 reveals a surprising coherence, and perhaps, above all, a continuity between indoors and out, between exteriors and furnished interiors. This is in part because McClean Design keeps closely involved in its projects from start to finish. "There are interior designers involved in quite a few of our projects," explains McClean, "but we tend to look at our houses as a whole. We don't do furniture, fixtures, and equipment. Things that are fixed to the building, on the other hand, we often do ourselves. We generally work with the same three or four interior designers, so there does tend to be a lot of consistency."

Blurring the Boundaries

The subtropical climate of Los Angeles and its relative dryness have facilitated development in the area of inventive, open houses. McClean readily inscribes his work in that tradition of openness in every sense, in both literal and figurative terms. "The overarching theme," he states, "is eliminating or blurring the boundaries between indoors and outdoors. The way we approach the buildings is that the materials flow from inside to outside. We suggest materials ourselves. The building comes with ideas about finishes and colors, and interior designers generally adapt to that, rather than us providing a kind of white box. We seek to create a unified, consistent feeling as one moves through the spaces, from exterior to interior." McClean keeps an even closer eye on the areas he does not directly control. McClean Design gets involved in lighting and built-in cabinetry, for example. "When the interior designer makes a presentation concerning the furnishings to be selected," says the architect, "that is a meeting I would be in, too. We work in a collaborative way. We see outside designers as an opportunity to enhance a project and not as a form of opposition to our work." McClean's clients usually defer to his suggestions not only for interior design choices, but also in the area of landscape architecture, where the firm's input is also taken into account by outside consultants.

Defining a Style

Paul McClean's careful attention to materials, detailing, landscape, and even beyond in, areas such as lighting aligns with his strong conviction that a house is meant to be lived in and is not to be an object that expresses the ego of the designer. Even the relatively muted colors that seem to dominate his work are the willful result of this attitude. "We do not often use bright colors in our work," says McClean. "We are in a desert environment where the light is very strong. I find that more muted tones are easier on the eye. We do try to make our houses blend in to the hillside and the natural environment. We don't necessarily want them to stand out." Though the houses of McClean Design have frequently been published in the professional press, they are not created to forward the reputation of the architect so much as they are to give the client a real home. "I think a house should be beautiful," says McClean, "but I don't want to make the kind of house that screams an architectural manifesto at you. We want the house to be the backdrop to your life. It should be a place of calmness and serenity—easy to use and practical. At the same time, the house should enhance your life. Architecture is a wonderful thing, but it is not all that life is about and sometimes architects forget that. It shouldn't get in the way."

Perhaps because he has been so focused on individual projects over the years, McClean did not set out to work in a specific style. In fact, he says, "I have become aware working on this book that we do have a style—I was not really aware of that before. I think that public buildings can have more of a presence, but a home needs to be a home. It has to be a place where residents are comfortable. My houses are not like the ones you see in magazines where there is a theme—like the Round House or the Black House. I think that concepts of that nature are inappropriate for homes. It should be about how the rooms are being perceived, how the volumes feel, how they relate to the outdoors. What is the light like in the room? What is the level of physical comfort? Those are the things that should drive the design of a house, not necessarily that the architect decided that the whole house should be white."

Avoiding Extremes

Perhaps the strongest feature of the style of Paul McClean, aside from his clean lines and strong connections between interiors and exteriors, is what might be called an absence of dogmatism, or perhaps the expression of a well-adjusted ego that does not need to impose itself on every design in a quirky or unrelenting way. It might even be that McClean views his work with a certain modesty—meaning not that his often large and luxurious homes are in themselves modest, but that the architect's real task is designing for others. He admits that Los Angeles is not frequently seen as being modest in its architectural expression. "Southern California," he says, "has been the crucible for residential design for the last hundred years. Los Angeles is a city that was built on fantasy. In a city that fabricated reality in a sense, private homes took a similar direction—people made Spanish haciendas, French chateaux, or Tudor houses, and all of those

Aerial view of Cuesta showing terraced gardens and water courtyard.

were built side by side. There is a fantasy component here, or a desire to experiment." When asked why he has never sought to avail himself of the experimental or conceptual side of his chosen city, or possibly why he cites Richard Meier and not Frank Gehry as a source of inspiration, McClean says, "I try to avoid the extremes. I find that some of Frank Gehry's homes are quite livable, but it also depends on the client. Some clients are more inclined to a conceptual house, as opposed to a house that is for living in. Some people are more experimental in their outlook, and that is where you get houses like the ones Gehry designed. The climate is forgiving, and that gives more room for experimentation."

It would seem apparent that the clients of McClean, often well-known people from the world of entertainment, are seeking not so much experimentation or the expression of architectural concepts as real homes with a sense of luxury. As he explains, part of the continuity seen in his designs is in response to the desire of clients to obtain results like those they have seen in earlier houses designed by the firm. Thus, the style that emerges from these houses is also borne of a certain collaboration between the architect, a limited number of chosen interior designers, and the clients themselves. Most of the clients of McClean Design come by word of mouth and more recently through images and descriptions seen on the Internet. People contact the firm with the idea of something they have already seen in mind. "We are trying to find materials that do give a sense of luxury," says McClean, "and also will hopefully be somewhat timeless. There tends to be some consistency from house to house as certain ideas work better than others and that information tends to get passed along. Clients often see something in a previous project and like to use it again if it is appropriate. We also like to encourage our clients and the interior designers we work with to take the houses in a different direction if possible, one that reflects our clients' taste rather than our own. But I do have to acknowledge that there is a certain continuity, much of which comes from the clients who have been drawn to us for both the architecture and the *materiality* of the homes. We do not try to impose a style on our clients. We let their own ideas complement the architecture."

The Value of Experience

The experience of practice over nearly twenty years has made the work of Paul McClean evolve. His success has brought him progressively larger and larger projects. This, of course, also speaks to the question of the arrival of new fortunes from abroad or from the tech industry, for example, and the taste for larger, more spectacular homes. McClean says, "My work has definitely evolved. As time has gone by there has been a programmatic evolution. We are seeing changes in the way people use homes. The homes I first worked on were two- to five-thousand square feet. Now most of the homes we design are averaging ten- to twelve-thousand square feet. The program changes as the homes get bigger. In Los Angeles, in places like Santa Monica or Culver City, there is a movement toward densification that is clear. On the other hand, people are also moving to suburbs and building bigger homes." Aside from issues of size, it seems clear that house design has evolved in other general ways that have an impact on the work of McClean Design. The architect states, "I hope the houses are getting more refined and better detailed. We are seeing things that are used or not used, and that helps us to learn. Technology is one of the biggest challenges. Lighting, for example, has become more and more complex with the different kinds of systems on offer. A room used to have a few lights; now there can be twenty or forty different ones."[5] Working with different size houses, right up to one of the largest residences built anywhere in recent years, McClean has shown flexibility and a capacity to adapt to changing times—qualities that not all architects have, especially those architects who prefer to keep using the same methods over the years. McClean is able to change with his clientele, and that is one reason that he is leaving a lasting mark in the area of residential design.

Beyond California

Paul McClean has focused his work largely in Los Angeles and the surrounding area. As the firm connects to more and more people through word-of-mouth and social media, it hopes to expand to work in other parts of the country and to work on other types of houses. "Going forward," McClean says, "I would love to do more homes in different environments, in real urban environments, or in rural locations where we can get away from hillside suburban lots. We are doing a large house right now that is near Vancouver on a 400-acre rural plot. The house relates to a lake on the site." Although the relative similarities between the sites where McClean has worked in Los Angeles have impacted his approach, he takes a typically upbeat position on his recent work. "Actually, the restrictions imposed by tight sites in Los Angeles sometimes permit the design to coalesce more quickly. There are a certain number of constraints that cannot be avoided," he says. "When you remove such restrictions from the discussion, you are almost left with a blank slate. You have to select points to relate to. In the case of the Vancouver house, it is a mountain. In Hawaii, we are designing another large house on a three-acre flat lot on the oceanfront. It is a house that forms a compound rather than a single building."

Rigor and Comfort

The plans of the houses of Paul McClean fully bear out his own thoughts about his work. There is often a simple and rigorous rectangular scheme at the base, and in some cases it forms the entire residence—the Oriole Way project is one example. Frequently, layer by layer and floor by floor, the plans becomes denser but they are still based on the same pattern. This is the case in the Temple Hills Drive house. Water features, always present, can also play a central role in a design, as in the Blue Jay Way house, where a water feature and spa, along with a long, rectangular infinity pool, slice through the residence and define its spaces. The plans are, of course, defined not only by programmatic requirements and budgets, but also by site constraints. An excellent example of McClean's reaction to an awkward triangular site was the Doheny Drive house with a sweeping curved façade and accompanying pool. Behind this great curve, the rest of the house assumes the more frequently seen rectangular layout favored by the architect. In one of the few houses published here that is not in California, the Whistler residence, the architect has literally built the structure into a steep, rocky site, but the basic floor plan is triangular.

The geometric forms employed correspond to McClean's desire to create homes that are both logical and comfortable. Unrestrained curvature and other forms inevitably generate lost spaces, and that is not the style of McClean. Although the houses are getting bigger and more luxurious, the basic idea of the architect remains—a kind of predictable solidity that is relayed by the choice of materials like stone as opposed to visible concrete, for example. Just as the plans are layered with an impeccable organizational logic, so, too, McClean adds layers of intent to the basic structure. Thus, water features, landscaping in harmony with the architecture, a strong sense of views and privacy, and even the decoration that he weighs in on, even though the office does not directly take into account moveable objects, all contribute to a coherent whole. The presence of water, often flowing over a wall or falling from a pool above, creates an introspective tone that is augmented by the architect's sense of the value of light. Water and light animate the houses of McClean and create a sense of peace within. The often relatively crowded circumstances of residential Los Angeles bring the architect to a style that is not distant from what is practiced in the densely urban environments of Japan. There, the presence of light, water, and wind is interpreted as the real presence of nature, even in places where the outside world is chaotic and unattractive. McClean

Rendering of a current project, an oceanfront family compound in the Kona District on the west side of the Big Island of Hawaii, 2020.

benefits from sites that have stunning views, so he adds a dimension that is not always present in even the most striking houses in Japan. The distant view—in particular when directed to the ocean beyond—also represents architectural use of the presence of nature, even in places where the city is all around. City views stretching for many miles are also spectacular in Los Angeles, so the site as it exists, augmented by manifestations of nature such as falling water, brings a sense of inner peace and harmony to a house of Paul McClean.

To Build a Real Home

Whether by choice or because clients demand it, well-known architects do not always master their work to the extent that Paul McClean does. They may allow interiors to be done without their input, preferring to give a signature form to a house rather than to worry about what some might consider the minutiae of design. McClean obviously follows his work from start to finish until a livable and, indeed, an exceptional home is delivered to his clients. This is a great quality in contemporary architecture, and one that seems increasingly rare. The ways in which McClean follows up on his designs, from start to finish, are also in keeping with his esthetic choices. The lines are crisp, the colors muted, and the ego of the architect is expressed more in his pride in creating a real home than in an interest in imposing his signature in a purely artistic way. The art here is in the totality of the work, not a dramatic sketch and an outlandish form. Walter Gropius and other founders of the Bauhaus imagined buildings that would be total works of art, the *Gesamtkunstwerk*, where an architect is responsible for the design and overseeing a building's totality—its shell, accessories, furnishings, and landscape. Gropius himself did not necessarily feel that the architect should do all of this, but he did believe that there should be an overriding esthetic sense involved. It might be said that others closer to the prototypical Southern California house, like Greene & Greene and Frank Lloyd Wright, were of this mind as well. McClean's plans and elevations have all the hallmarks of modernity, and he certainly defines his projects as being that of overall mastery of a building, from sketch to completed home. He works with a group of contractors, interior designers, and landscape designers who know his sensibility and who logically contribute to creating a complete end product. From the interior serenity afforded by the presence of light, water, and coherent materiality, the gaze and the mind of the resident are then transported elsewhere. Might it be here that the goal is not so much to create a complete work of art as it is to build a real home, a home in keeping with the aspirations and means of clients who can readily perceive the splendor of a night view of Los Angeles? With an infinity pool that allows the gaze to move without barrier from the plane of daily existence to a scale that makes even the powerful feel small, McClean is also not a simple designer of predictable forms. He has the ambition to generate exceptional spaces that also function as comfortable homes and that ultimately transport the resident to a place of contemplation of what lies beyond, of the all-important view.

Despite the number of houses that McClean has designed in Los Angeles, it is clear that the method and style of the architect can be applied elsewhere, for example, in the large residences he was building in Hawaii and Vancouver as this book went to press. These houses quite simply fit into their context just as the ones in Los Angeles designed by McClean do. They may spread over a larger area because the sites and programs allow a more generous use of space, but they share with their Angeleno predecessors the same sense of space, of layering, of modernity, materiality, and comfort. In fact, these qualities are not specific to Los Angeles or any other place. The point is to design houses that fit into their sites and that offer attention to detail in every aspect, emphasizing quality and generating a feeling of inner serenity at the same time they encourage residents to lift their eyes and to dream about things that are greater than they are. The houses of Paul McClean are conceived in an integral way, from site and structure to materials and views. They are coherent. Much as Wright and Lautner had it, real architecture is about "the whole idea."

Philip Jodidio
Lausanne
June 2, 2018

[1] Aaron Betsky, "Horatio West Court Packs Feel of Openness, Form Into Dense Space," *Los Angeles Times*, June 13, 1991. http://articles.latimes.com/1991-06-13/news/we-937_1_horatio-west-court accessed June 1, 2018.

[2] John Lautner interviewed by Marlene Laskey, "Responsibility, Infinity, Nature," Oral History Program, UCLA, 1986. https://ia802707.us.archive.org/20/items/responsibilityin00laut/responsibilityin00laut.pdf accessed June 1, 2018.

[3] A.K. Thomson, "Prices of Houses in Los Angeles Hit a New High," November 10, 2017, *Financial Times*, https://www.ft.com/content/065caba4-bffe-11e7-823b-ed31693349d3 accessed May 30, 2018. Andrew Khouri, "Southern California Home Prices Jump to a Record High," *Los Angeles Times*, April 23, 2018. http://www.latimes.com/business/la-fi-home-prices-20180423-story.html accessed May 30, 2018.

[4] Paul McClean, e-mail to the author, June 1, 2018.

[5] This quote and the others in the text from Paul McClean are from an e-mail sent to the author in response to written questions on May 7, 2018, and a telephone interview on May 9, 2018.

VIA MAJORCA

Completed in January 2008, this house is located in Laguna Beach, a seaside resort in the southern part of Orange County. Built on a tight 6,468-square-foot lot for a family of four, not far from the ocean, this is the smallest house featured in this book. Unlike most McClean Design houses, the Via Majorca house was built on a flat site where, per the architect, "view considerations were not a priority." The long, narrow rear yard was imagined by the architects to be a kind of outdoor room connected to the family room and the kitchen. Sliding doors allow the main living space to be directly connected to the garden. A kitchen island is matched with a similar outdoor island, again affirming the connection between the indoors and the exterior spaces. The curving metal façade of the house was somewhat controversial before construction, but McClean Design succeeded in presenting the project as part of a general transition in the architecture of the immediate area. The lines of the façade correspond to the curvature of the cul-de-sac drive in front of the house. The rest of the house is completely orthogonal. A linear skylight over the sliding doors in the living spaces and clerestory windows in the entry bring natural light from the front of the house into the living spaces. Paul McClean states, "A strong palette of black and silver metal, charcoal and gray stone, and dark stained cabinetry provide a calm sense of order and help to highlight the owners' strategic use of art and planting, which provide color." Exterior walls are clad in zinc metal composite wall panels, while interior walls are in Sienna Silver and Paradigm travertine and Colombino limestone.

Opposite: A full story glass lantern is to the right of the front door.
Following double page: The rear garden is designed to be an extension of the main living space.

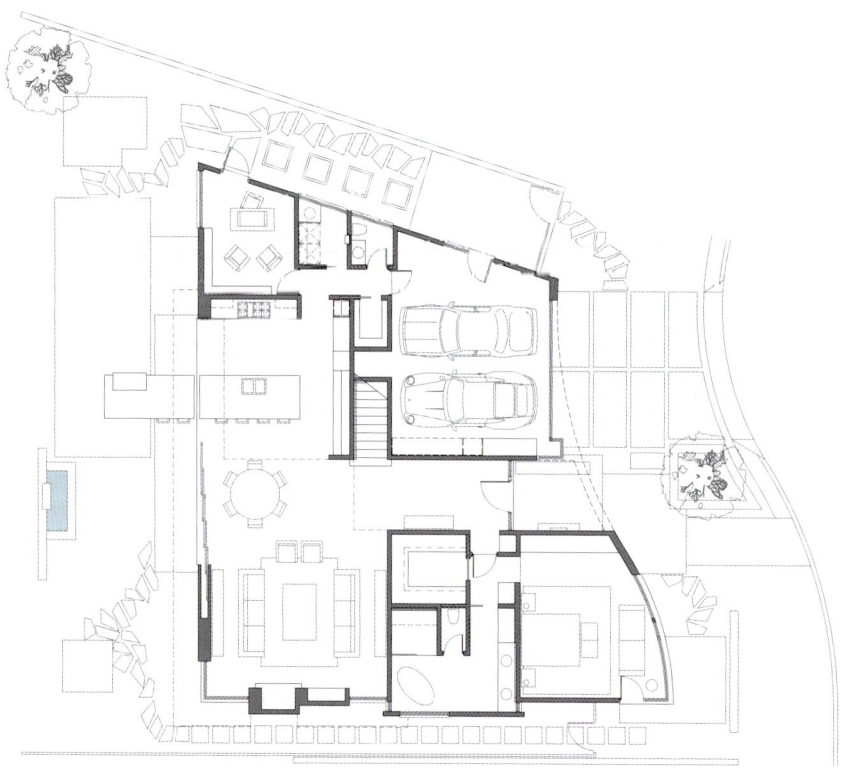

MAIN LEVEL PLAN

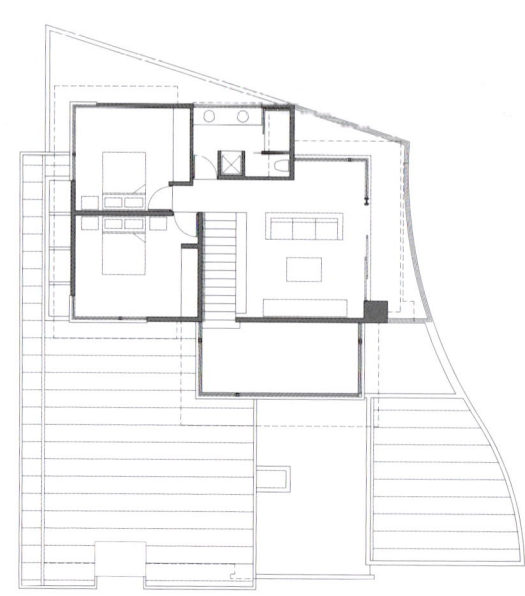

UPPER LEVEL PLAN

SECTIONS

BLUE JAY WAY

This was the first substantial project undertaken by McClean Design in Los Angeles. Set on a 13,357-square-foot lot in the Bird Streets area of the city, a neighborhood often associated with musicians and movie stars. Unusually, this house is bisected by a pool and water feature in response to the client's request for a seventy-five-foot-long pool, a constraint that the architect says he used to imagine the residence as a "canyon, deep and narrow with a river running through it." The pool begins with a water wall near the entry and ends with an "infinity drop-off to the city lights beyond" at the opposite side of the site above Sunset Strip. Full height glazing allows residents to relish the view and emphasizes the indoor-outdoor design, which takes full advantage of the local climate. The pool also bisects the functions of the house, with the private spaces, including the master bedroom and a study, on one side and the public ones on the other. The entry bridge spans the pool and connects the two wings. A clerestory window marks the main stair, which descends to a secondary bridge over the pool that connects the lower level garage to the guest rooms and media area. There are three guest rooms on the lower level. These bedrooms have openings to the rear garden and the pool. The lower level also has an outdoor terrace and lounging area. The plan for the 7,000-square-foot residence was the result of close collaboration with the original client. The house was sold and extensively remodeled by McClean Design in 2016 at the request of the new owner, Tim Bergling, known under the stage name Avicii. The remodeling included the addition of a recording studio and accessory spaces on the lower level, created by reclaiming part of the existing four-car garage. The reworking of the house also included extensive changes to the finishes. The overall design can be described as crisp and comfortable, with clearly defined edges and surfaces. The material palette includes Negro Marquina marble and Alcazar Portico slate on exterior walls; the same marble was used on interior walls. Floors are oak plank and Super Thassos (white glass). The house is shielded from the street by dense vegetation, assuring the privacy of the owner.

Opposite: Much of the home is screened from the street with only the cantilevered dining room visible from below.
Following double page: The signature design element is the water feature and pool that bisects the program of the house.

"THE GLAZED ENTRY BRIDGE IS A TRULY UNIQUE SPACE, TRAVERSING THE WATER FEATURE CANYON AND HOVERING BETWEEN THE TWO WINGS OF THE HOUSE, WHICH ARE FOCUSED EXCLUSIVELY ON THE CITY VIEW."

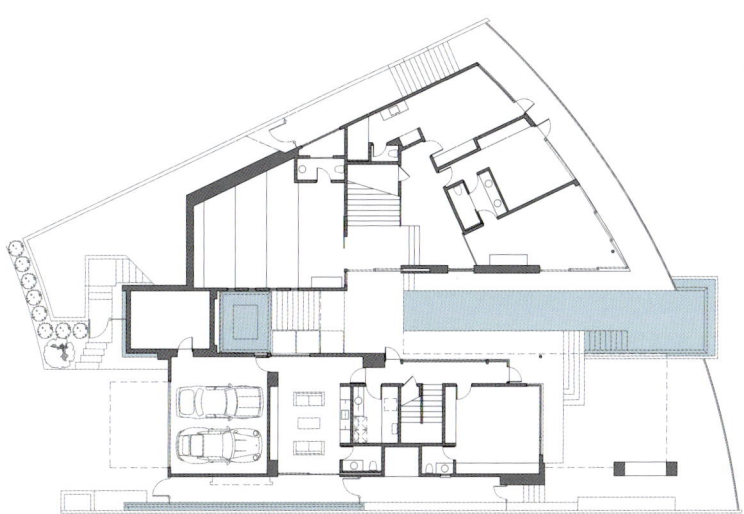

BASEMENT LEVEL PLAN

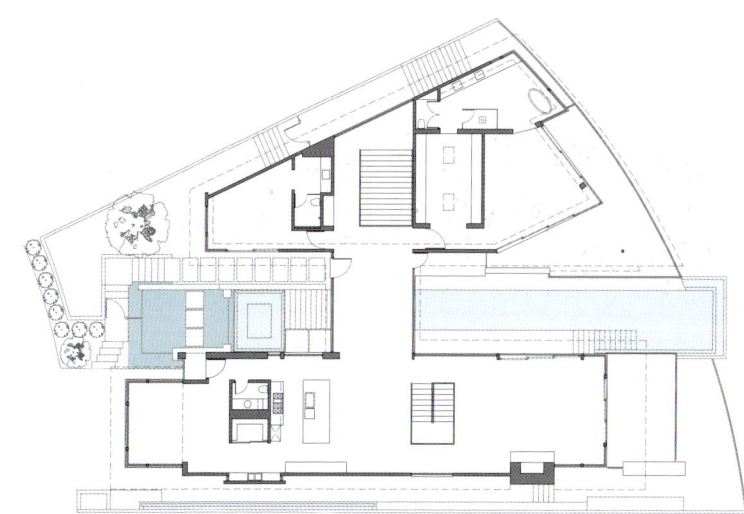

MAIN LEVEL PLAN

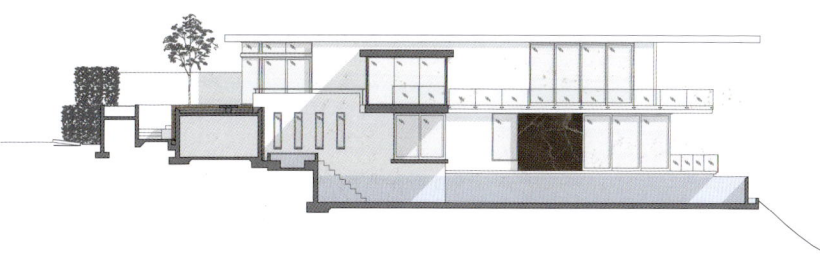

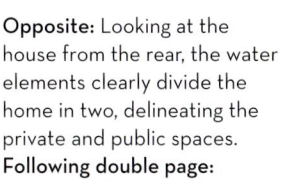

Opposite: Looking at the house from the rear, the water elements clearly divide the home in two, delineating the private and public spaces.
Following double page: The water features can be compared to a river in a canyon with bridging elements such as the entry connecting the two halves of the home.

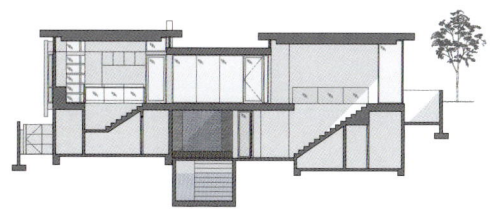

SECTIONS

Opposite: At night the home lights up like a jewel box with clear visibility of the components and the view, while privacy is maintained from the street.

SARBONNE

Sarbonne Road is in the Bel Air area, north of the Bel-Air Country Club. Completed in September 2011 for Nile Niami, this 14,000-square-foot residence is located on a steep 45,495-square-foot lot with limited area for building. According to the architect, "When we first met with Nile, we all agreed the challenge was to get the driveway as high as possible so that the distance to the front door would not be too great and the house could be placed high enough to take advantage of the views." The approach to the residence is through a circular vehicle court near the four-car garage at the basement level. A curved staircase rises up from the court to the main level. The two-story entrance stands above this court and leads to the living room, dining room, and wine wall display, a library/office, a family room, the kitchen, a media room near a small bedroom, a spa, and an infinity edge pool, all on the main level. A long hallway clad with gray striated marble walls acts as a spine for the main rooms and also serves to bring in natural light on both sides through the use of smaller outdoor spaces against the hill. A spiral staircase curves up from the living space to the upper level, where the master bedroom suite is located together with an office, three smaller bedrooms, and a guest suite that includes a living room and another bedroom. A gym and balcony also are on the upper floor. The outdoor deck is extended over the slope to improve privacy vis-à-vis the houses below and to increase the available living space. The architect explains, "Along the southern façade, the polished white-colored stone from the interior is carried outside to form an expansive deck. Beyond the deck, an overly long infinity lap pool frames the view and contains a seemingly floating fire feature." Concludes the architect, "The result is a modern urban haven that 'floats' above the city below."

Opposite: A narrow pool and water feature accentuate the long lines of the home. **Following double page.** The firepit seating area of the house fully accentuates the view.

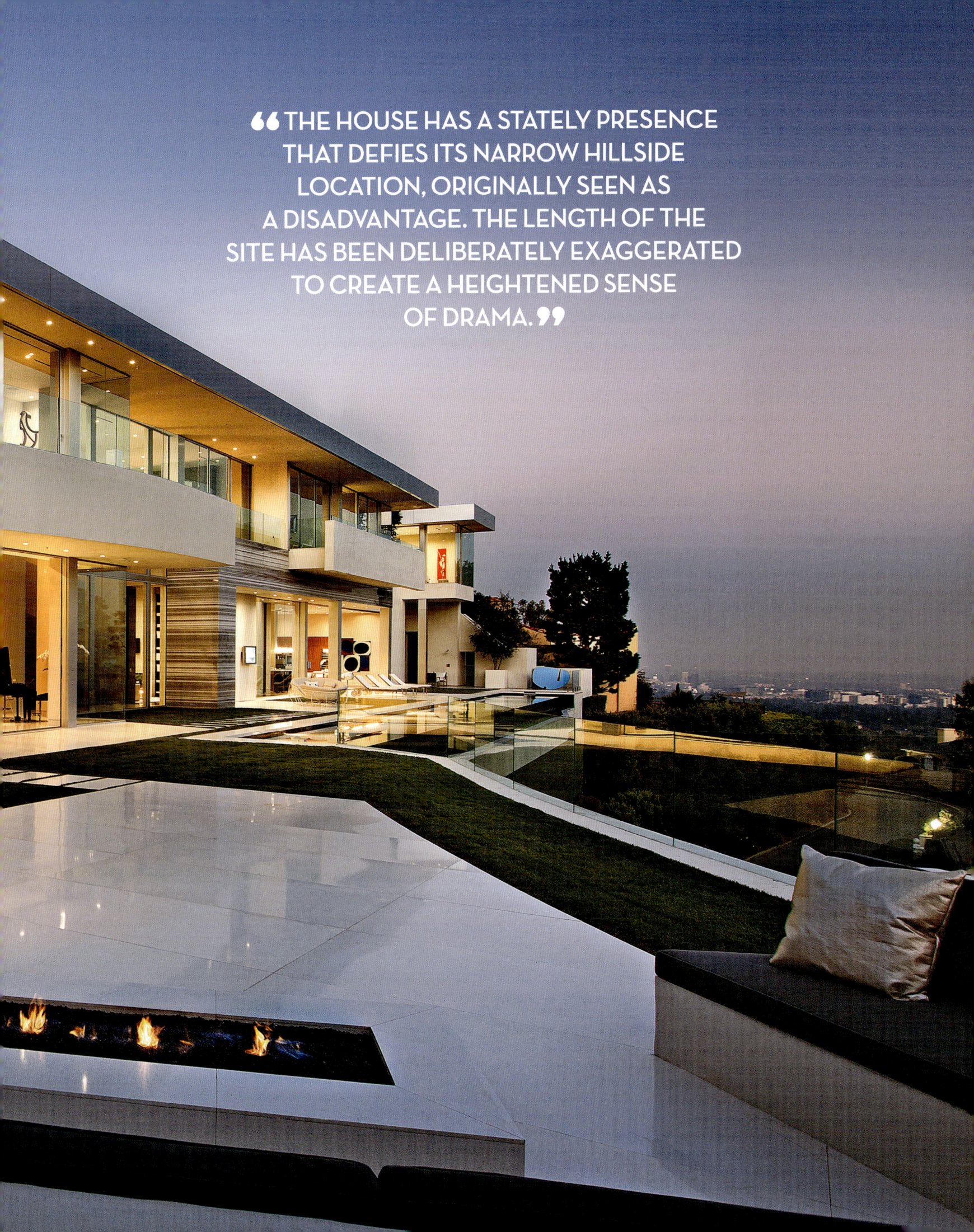

"THE HOUSE HAS A STATELY PRESENCE THAT DEFIES ITS NARROW HILLSIDE LOCATION, ORIGINALLY SEEN AS A DISADVANTAGE. THE LENGTH OF THE SITE HAS BEEN DELIBERATELY EXAGGERATED TO CREATE A HEIGHTENED SENSE OF DRAMA."

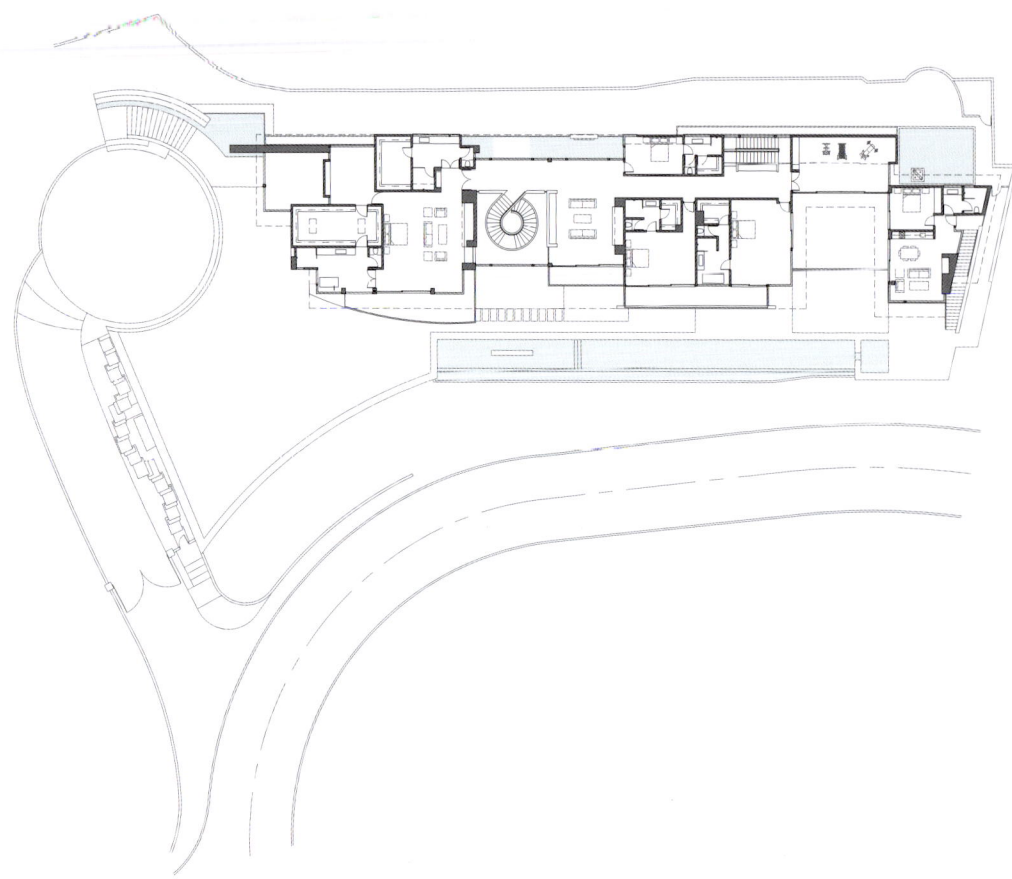

UPPER LEVEL PLAN

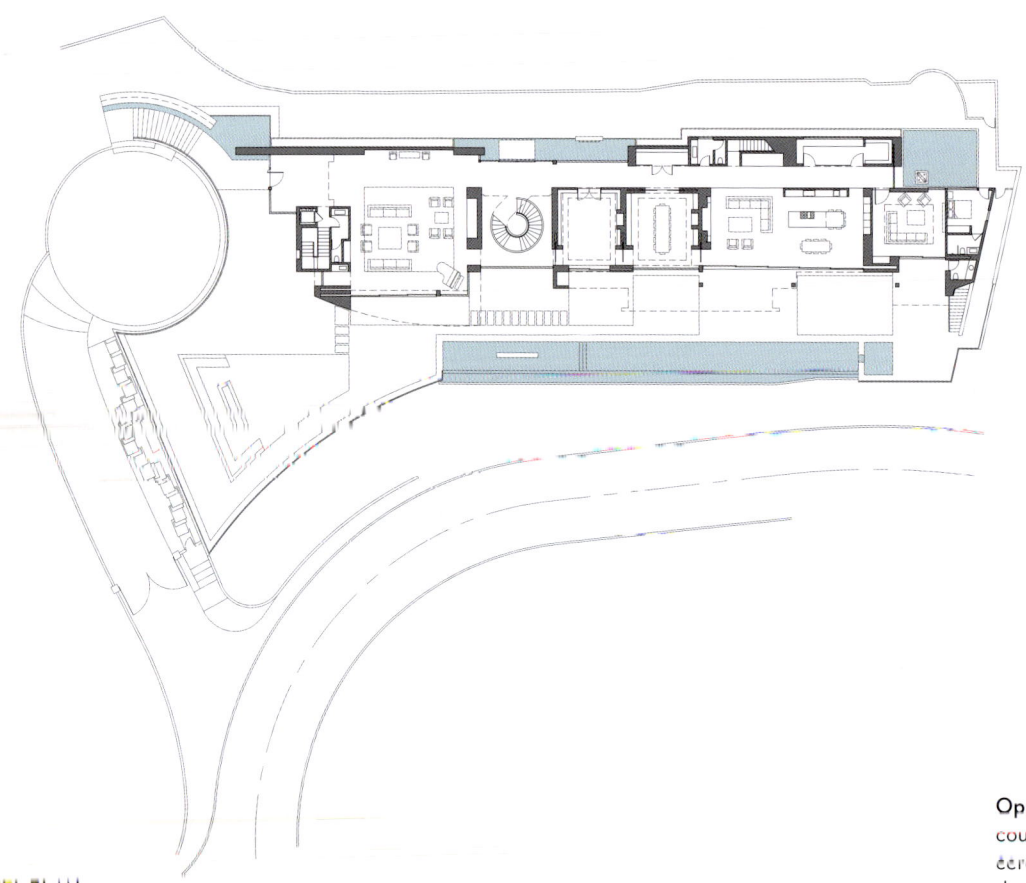

MAIN LEVEL PLAN

Opposite: The curving drive court staircase creates a ceremonial approach to the double-height entrance.

Opposite: The family room opens to the pool and terrace, creating a continuous fluid space.
Below: The material palette of the master bath is warm and inviting.
Following double page: The spiral stair is a signature design element of the project, as is the spine corridor connecting all the ground floor spaces.

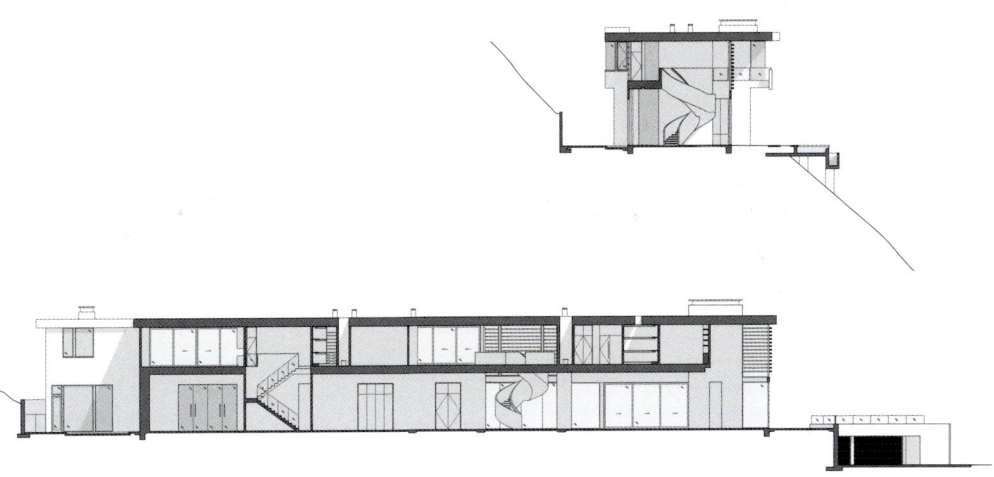

SECTIONS

ORIOLE DRIVE

Oriole Drive is one of the Bird Streets located above the Sunset Strip in West Hollywood. This house was completed in October 2012 on a 53,064-square-foot lot in place of an earlier home. The project was designed for Dean McKillen and Nile Niami, who co-developed the property. The property offers views to the west side of Los Angeles and the ocean beyond. The entry sequence of the new residence "overlays the original, and certain aspects of the floor plan match the original home," according to the architect. The basement level of the house includes bedrooms, a patio, a gym, and a studio. The main level has the family, living, and entertainment spaces, as well as a guest house, a large glazed garage where classic cars are displayed, and, outdoors, an infinity pool. The media room on this floor has a hidden projection system that allows movies to be viewed inside or outside. A double-height atrium art gallery space that admits ample natural light leads to the two-story living room. The master bedroom is set on the uppermost level of the residence. The main materials used are wood and mocha-colored marble. Numerous water features enliven the house in a style similar to that of other houses by McClean Design. A single water element connects the main house to the glass garage and guest house, as well as cascading down to the gym below, unifying the components of the site. Paul McClean explains, "An interesting side note is that the house is on the footprint of an earlier Ricardo Legorreta house designed for the actor Ricardo Montalbán and his wife, Georgiana Young. Our original intention was to remodel and expand it. We struggled hard with this, the existing plan being insular and private and somewhat the opposite of what our clients wished. After several rounds of design, we abandoned the idea of a remodel at our clients' request and embarked on a new approach, although the entry sequence contains ghosts of the original design and the house is much the better for it."

Opposite: A bronze sculpture acts as a focal point at the end of a long vista near the pool.
Following double page: The family room crosses over the water feature, providing views in both directions.

"THE WATER FEATURE IS CRITICAL TO CONNECTING AND UNIFYING THE DISPARATE ELEMENTS OF THE PROJECT WHILE DRAWING THE USER TO THE VIEW, WHICH IS ONLY AVAILABLE FROM THE FAR END OF THIS DEEP LOT."

Opposite: The main two-story living space is separated from the more intimate adjoining family area by a long linear fireplace.

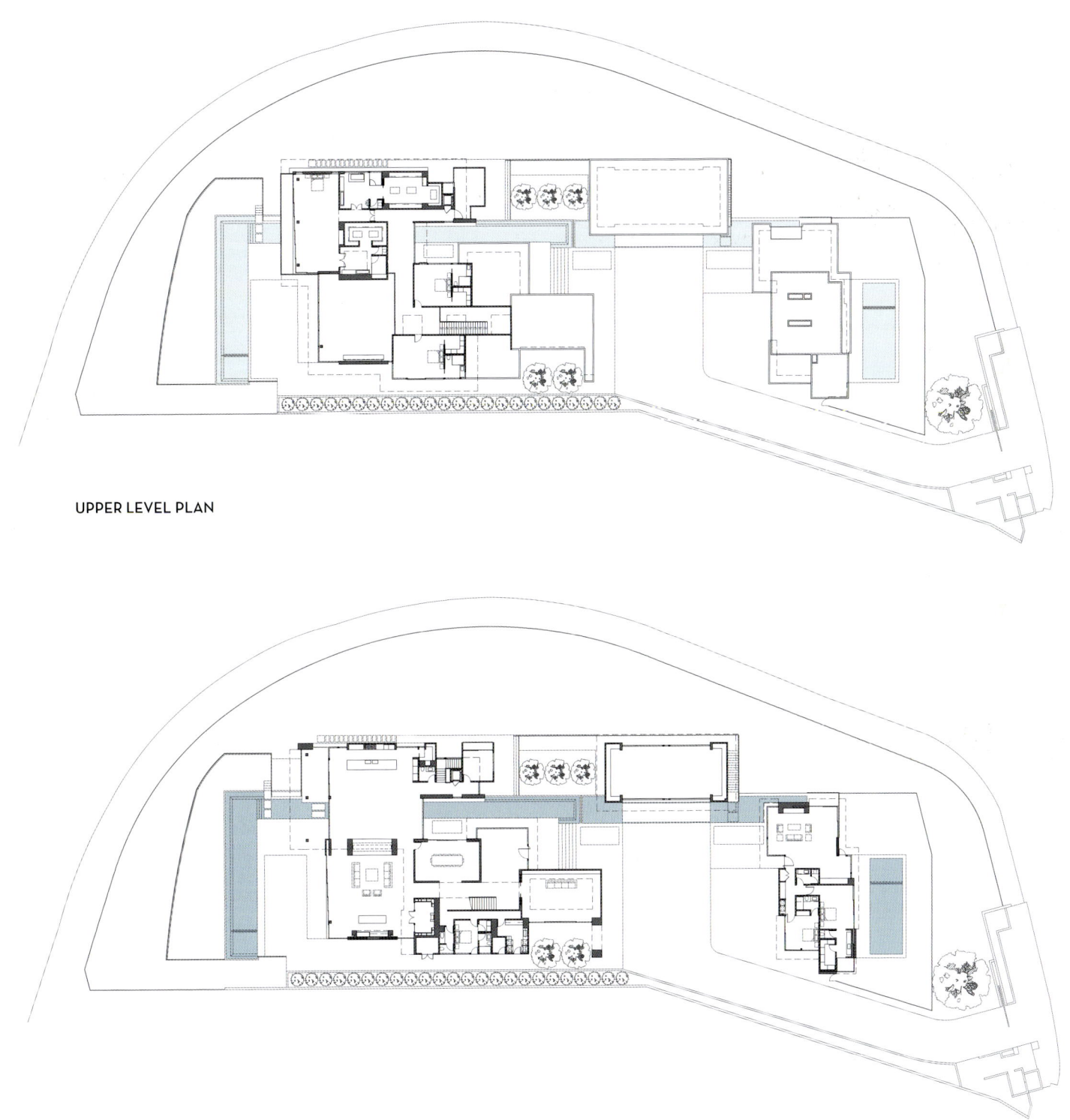

UPPER LEVEL PLAN

MAIN LEVEL PLAN

Opposite: Glass walls throughout the home can be easily retracted to connect with outdoor spaces.
Following double page: The water feature connects all three volumes on the lot but is at its most dramatic near the entry to the home.

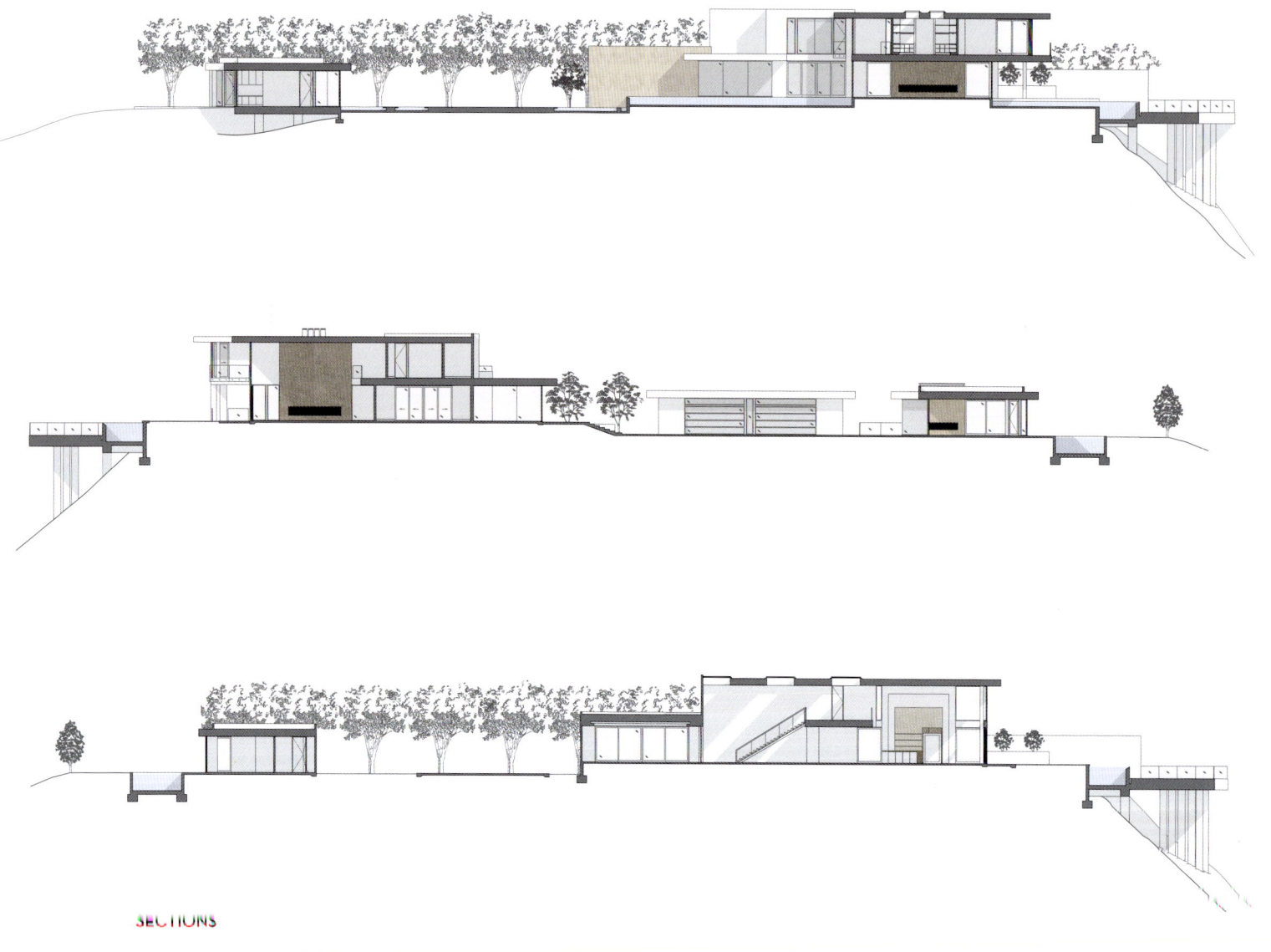

SECTIONS

61

ORIOLE WAY

Oriole Way is a small street high in the Bird Streets of Los Angeles that overlooks the Sunset Strip. Built on a very steep 17,244-square-foot lot, this house was completed in October 2012 in collaboration with Nile Niami. The parking area and garage are located at the top of the site, where there is easier access to the street, with the actual entry at the middle level of the house utilizing the street's continuous slope to avoid the need for a high entry stair. Residents and visitors enter the double-height living space from an entry courtyard with a water-feature. The dining room opens to the water garden of the three-story house. Because of the nature of the site, each level has panoramic views of downtown Los Angeles. The basic design of the house is rectangular with two bedrooms, a wine room, a gym, and media and A/V rooms on the basement level and the pedestrian entry, living, dining, and kitchen areas, a family room, a master bedroom, a spa and an infinity pool on the main level. The basement hallway was widened to create a gallery for art with the wine room located at its far end. The upper level, which is at street level, includes the garage and a guest room. A rooftop deck above the master bedroom with a reflecting pool—a sky mirror—is the focus of this upper floor. The color palette of the house ranges from white to tan, with some darker notes from wood and carpet. The house appears to be perched on the edge of a cliff; special attention was paid to creating a useable outdoor terrace and locating all the primary rooms on one level.

Opposite: The entire mid-level of the home opens to the pool terrace and to the views beyond.
Following double page: Double-height spaces are rare in this area due to height restrictions, but this site allowed for the creation of a dramatic living space.

> "A QUINTESSENTIALLY URBAN HOUSE THAT IS BOTH PART OF AND ABOVE THE CITY BELOW, THIS HOUSE IS ALL ABOUT L.A."

Opposite: Looking down from the loft toward the pool terrace and the view of the city beyond.

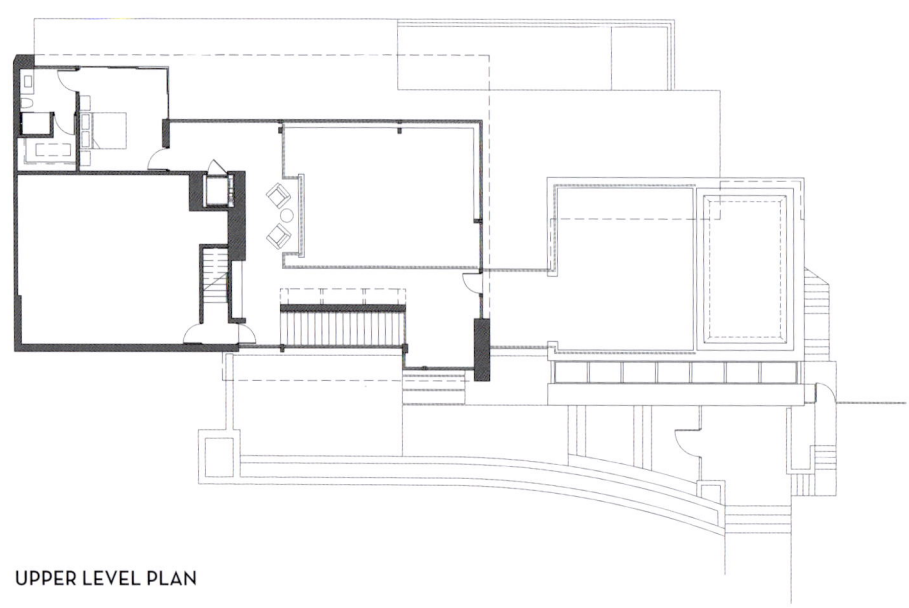

UPPER LEVEL PLAN

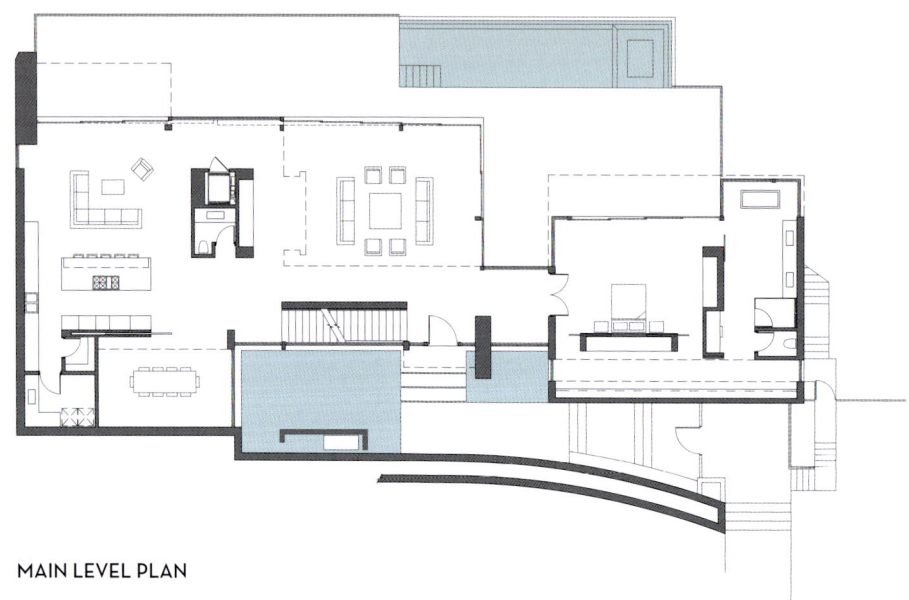

MAIN LEVEL PLAN

SECTIONS

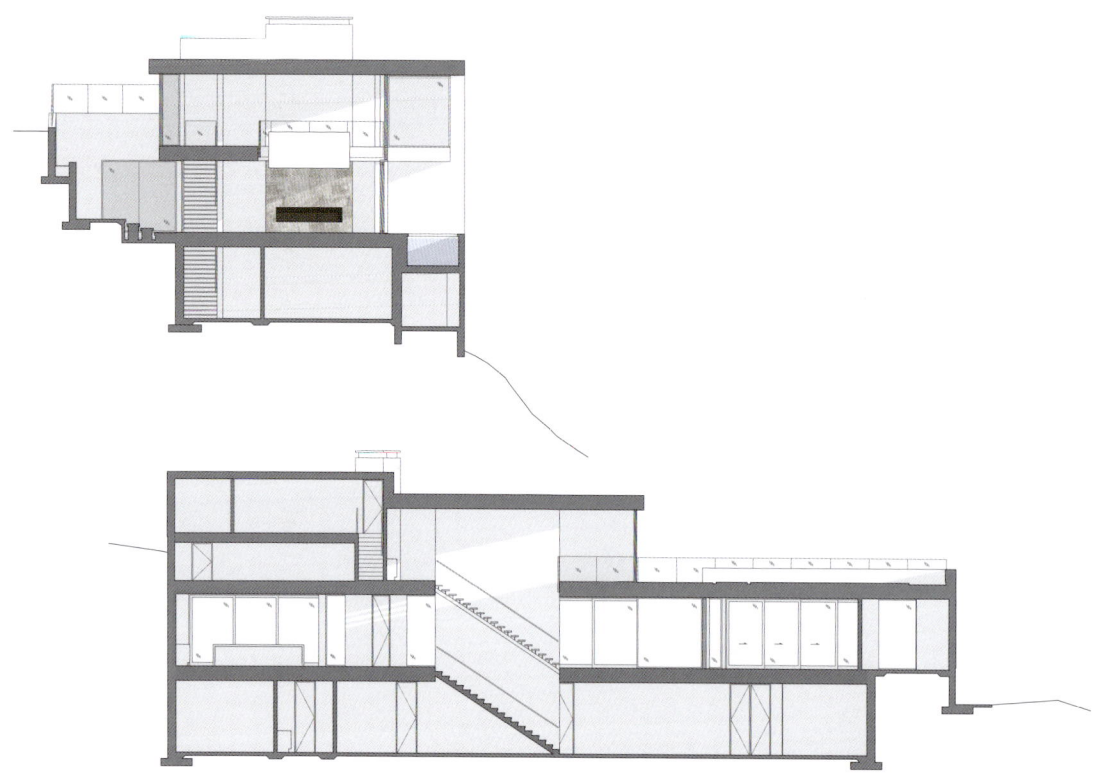

SAN VICENTE

Completed in April 2013, this house, currently owned by an art collector, is located on San Vicente Boulevard in the Brentwood area of Los Angeles. The lot measures 31,466 square feet and does not offer a view, meaning that the residence is more focused on its garden. Because of traffic on the street, visual and noise buffers in the form of a landscape barrier, high gates, and a curved glass wall became a design priority. The wall leads to a waterfall used for further noise abatement and an infinity edge decorative pool. The double-height entrance has formal dining and living rooms on either side. A floating glass staircase overlooks an herb garden behind the kitchen. The architect explains, "The kitchen is truly the heart of the home and opens radially into the family room and breakfast area with views to the garden and kitchen garden beyond." The main level of the house with the motor court and entry includes a media room, an entertainment bar, the living room, dining room and kitchen, an office, and the garage. Four bedrooms and the master bedroom suite are situated on the upper floor. A unique feature is the master bedroom terrace glass floor, which is located over the outdoor living space, bringing extra natural light into the central kitchen area. The rear garden of the house, where the pool is located, has a pool house with a roof whose curvature echoes that of the roof of the main house. The primary public day-to-day living spaces and bedrooms face away from the road, with only the formal spaces opposite the front water garden. The house is finished in cool Athens Grey limestone with light plaster and paint tones and bronze metal accents to provide a "warm casual atmosphere for family living." White walls and black window frames sharply delineate the volumes of the residence. When the current owners bought the house, they worked with the architect to make small but meaningful changes so that it would better suit their family—and those changes have improved the home, according to the architect.

Opposite: The entry courtyard leads directly to the heart of the home and the garden beyond.
Following double page: The living room and kitchen connect to the garden spaces in an open and informal way.

Opposite: The entry courtyard is designed to provide audible and visual privacy from the street beyond.

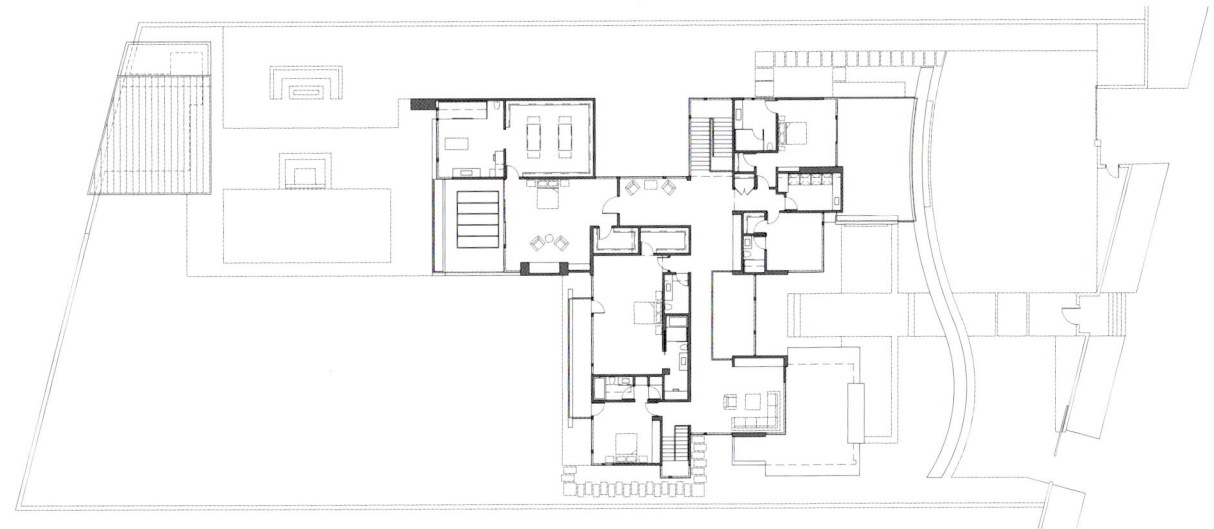

UPPER LEVEL PLAN

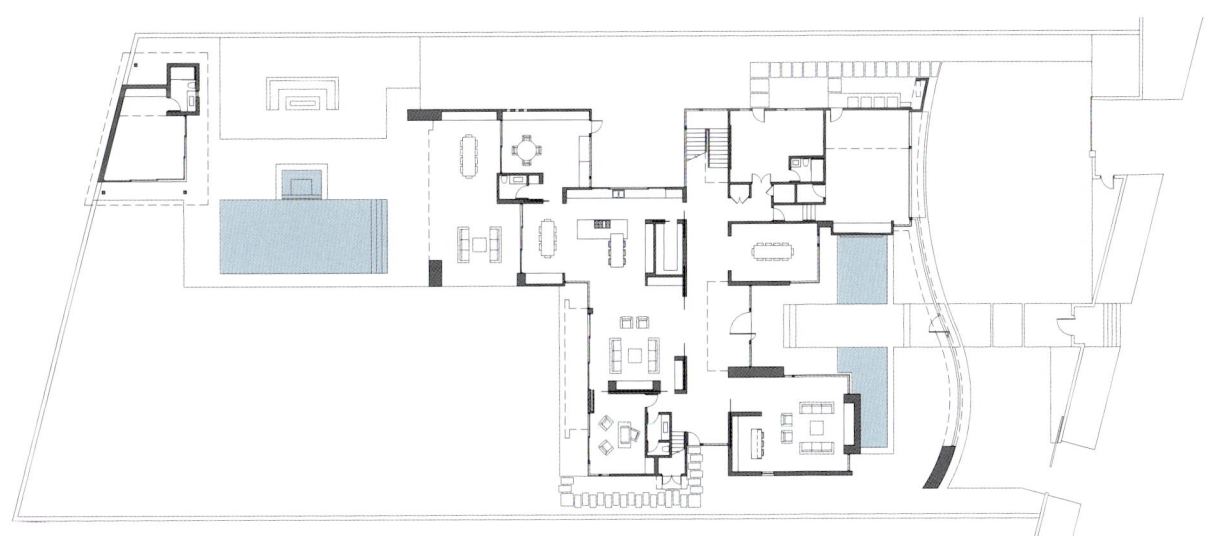

MAIN LEVEL PLAN

Opposite: The covered outdoor terrace adjacent to the pool is the real center of the house.
Below: The guest house acts as a focal point within the garden.
Following double page: The material and color palette of the house is soft, warm, and inviting.

SECTIONS

83

Opposite: By pushing the house closer to the street, the architect was able to create a large garden that acts as a haven of calm for the owners.

CARLA RIDGE

Carla Ridge is a road in the Trousdale Estates area of Beverly Hills, known for the homes of such residents as Jennifer Aniston and Elvis Presley. The Carla Ridge house was completed on a 24,451-square-foot site in July 2014 for the developer Nile Niami, who purchased the plans from Paul McClean's original client and was heavily involved in the material palette of the home. The project presented a certain number of zoning issues, such as restrictions that do not allow basements to have views, nor for construction to be extended beyond the existing level pad. The new design creates a courtyard that brings light into the basement. With natural light brought in this way, it was possible to create two bedrooms facing the courtyard's olive tree, whose presence offers a contrast to the crisp architecture. The entry path crosses a transparent glass bridge and a water feature that spills down to the basement, further animating the lower level. The floating staircase leading down to the basement looks out on a secondary light well, also designed to enhance the lower living area. At the main level an infinity pool connects the house, inside and outside, to the city views beyond. The overhangs to the rear of the house create spaces that are at once covered and outdoors, in keeping with the California lifestyle. The roofs over the master bedroom and family areas are lowered to "create more intimate spaces," McClean says. The house has an overall silver and marble palette, with the exception of the midnight-blue entry gate. The 4,814-square-foot basement level includes media and family space, three bedrooms, and a gym. Kitchen, dining, and living areas, as well as the master bedroom, are on the main level, which has a floor area of 5,181 square feet. The architect states, "This was one of the first houses to employ a basement-level light well, a design approach we continue to explore in many of our current homes."

Opposite: The house is perceived as a floating glass pavilion from the entry.
Following double page: A view from the pool, looking back towards the great room.

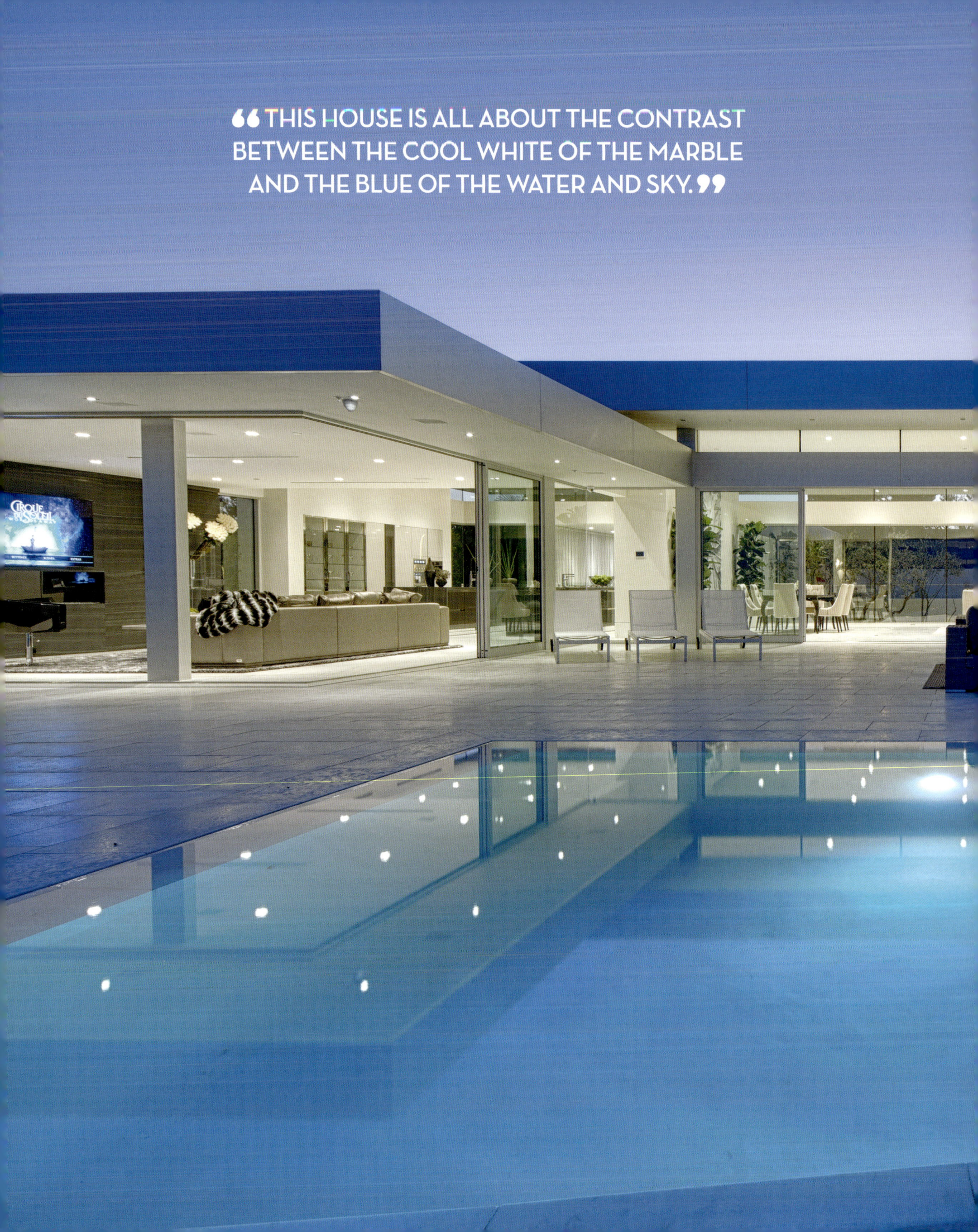

"THIS HOUSE IS ALL ABOUT THE CONTRAST BETWEEN THE COOL WHITE OF THE MARBLE AND THE BLUE OF THE WATER AND SKY."

MAIN LEVEL PLAN

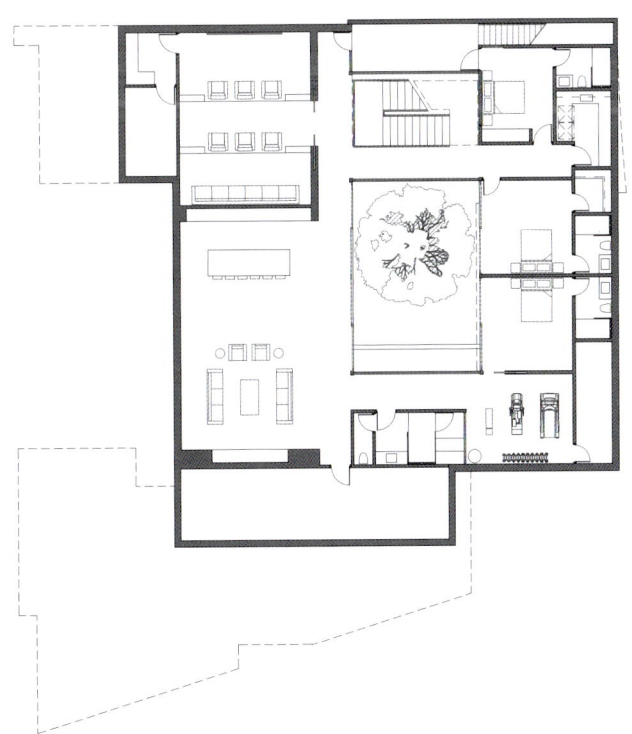

BASEMENT LEVEL PLAN

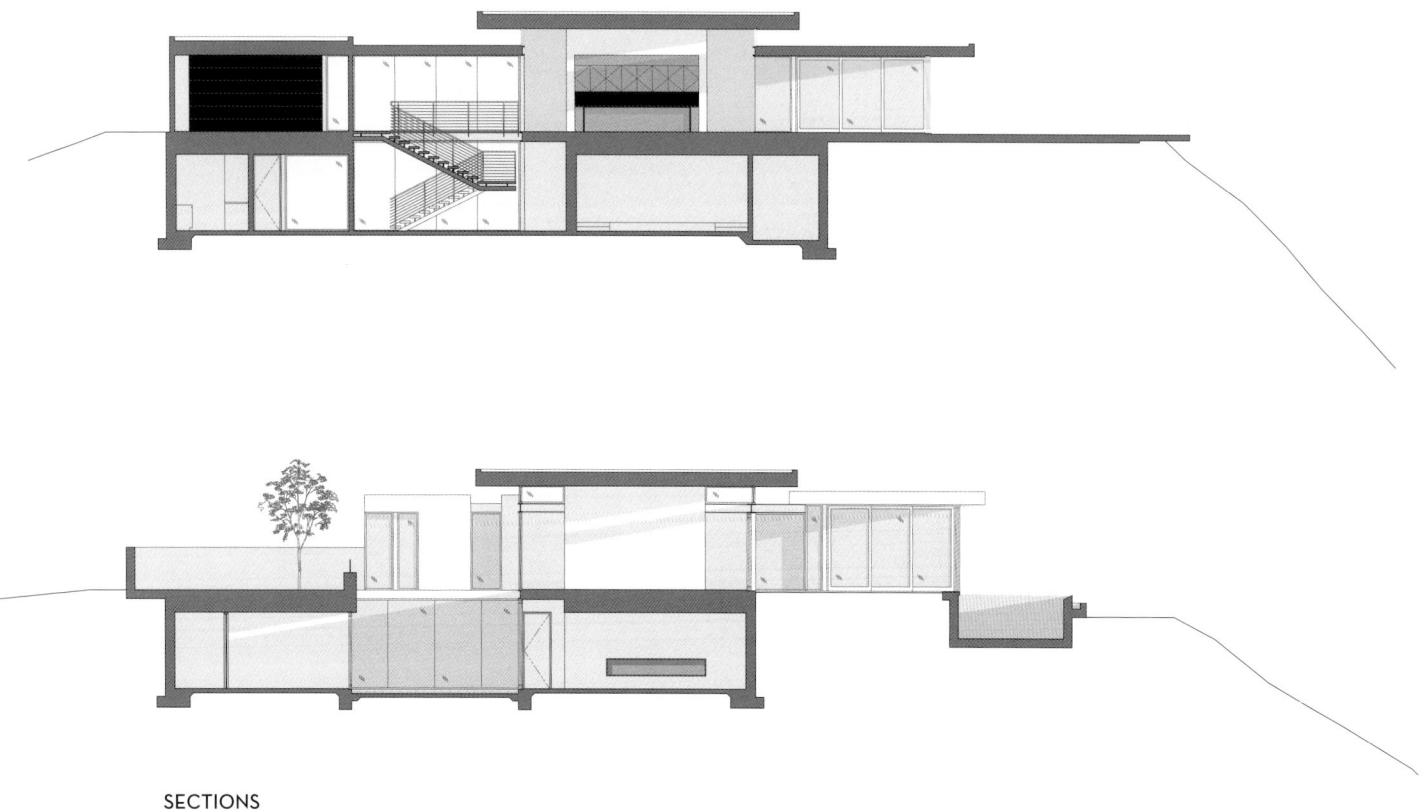

SECTIONS

Opposite: The central courtyard floods the areas below grade with natural light.

TEMPLE HILLS

Local zoning restrictions required the roof of this house, completed in September 2014, to be below the street to preserve views from neighboring properties. The architect states, "This turned out to be an advantage, allowing us to locate the garage in a sub-basement on the lower street, thereby increasing the available space for gardens and living space at the upper level." The entry below the street level also minimizes noise from above and allows residents and visitors quite literally to leave the busy street behind as they enter the house. The 7,891-square-foot site of the house is about half a mile inland from the ocean in Laguna Beach. A waterfall helps to screen noise from the street. Smaller than most homes by McClean Design (3,000 square feet), the house has a sloped, curving roof that "mimics surrounding rolling hills." The curved deck of the house in its turn makes reference to the waves visible in the distance. The basement level is essentially given over to the garage, with a light-filled stairwell leading up to the main floor. An elevator also serves the house, given the steep nature of the site. On the lower level, there are two bedrooms, a family room, and a garden terrace. The main level, where the entry is located, has living, dining, and kitchen space, the master bedroom, and a large viewing deck. All rooms in the house have views of the ocean. The design assumes that it is possible for the owners to live essentially on this floor as they get older, employing the elevator to descend to the garage. The architect also succeeded in giving a good deal of privacy to this house, designed for a couple, which is quite close to neighboring residences and the upper road.

Opposite: The house appears to float above the site at sunrise.
Following double page: View from the main living room to the ocean vista beyond.

" THE PALETTE FOR THIS HOUSE IS BASED ON THE OWNERS' CONCEPT OF STORMY SKIES, THE EVER-CHANGING SKYSCAPE OF THE OCEAN BELOW THAT CONTINUES TO FASCINATE THEM. "

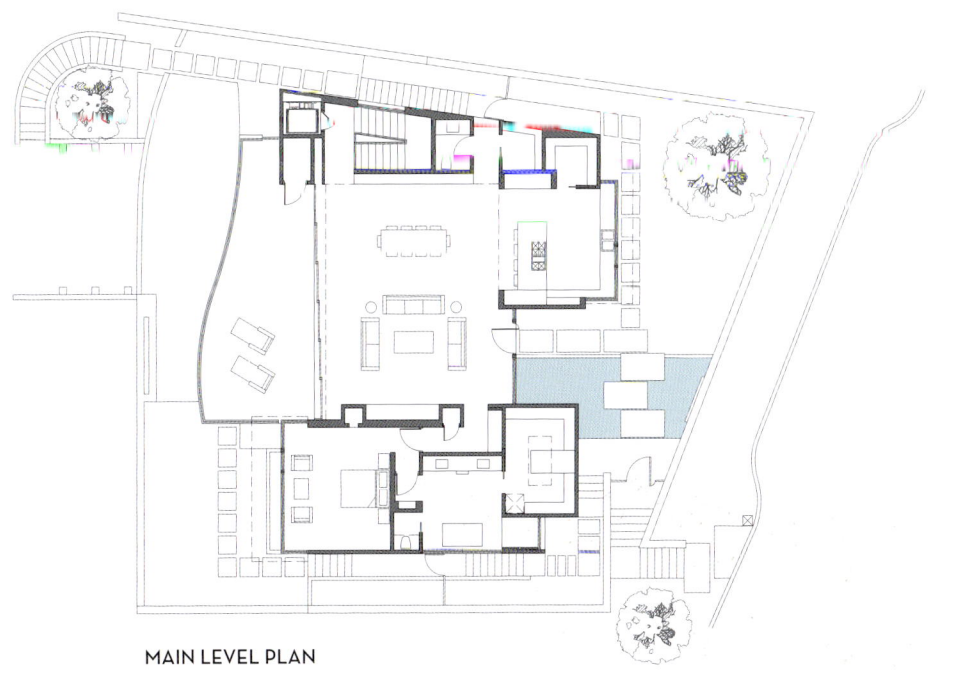

MAIN LEVEL PLAN

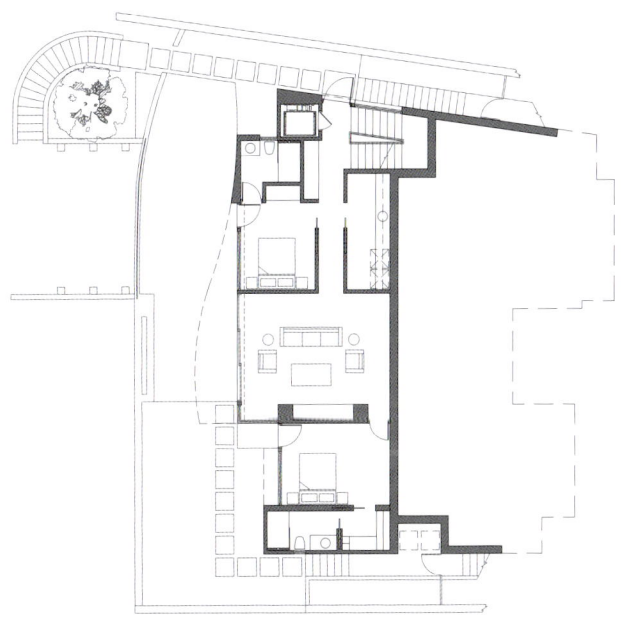

LOWER LEVEL PLAN

Opposite: The kitchen connects with the dining and living area to provide a single fluid living space.

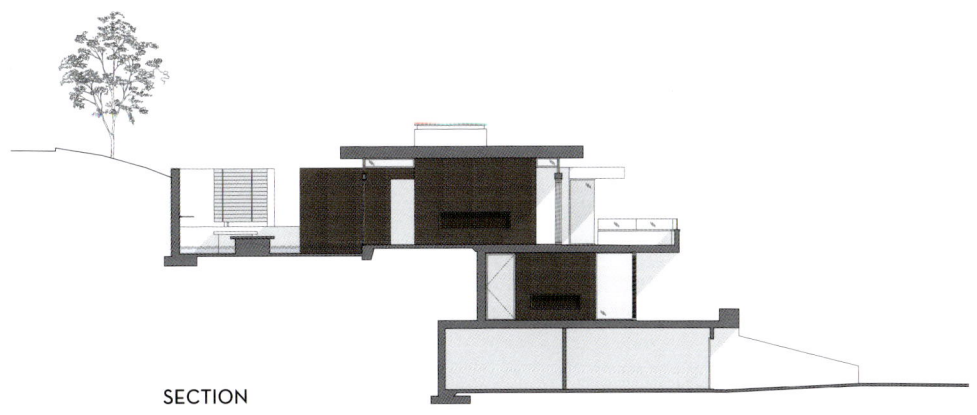

SECTION

TANAGER III

Built for Dean McKillen, son of the Irish property developer Patrick "Paddy" McKillen on a 16,717-square-foot corner lot, this residence was completed in October 2014 on Thrasher Avenue in the Bird Streets north of Sunset Boulevard. This is the third house designed by the architect on this exclusive street. It is currently the property of a well-known fashion designer for whom the architect recently remodeled the house. The unusual shape of the lot, with a narrow, triangular rear limit and houses directly below, made careful placement necessary. The entrance to the house is walled off from the street. Visitors then take in the house and the view as they walk across a bridge opening to a water courtyard below and centered on the city view. The basement level of the house includes the garage, an office, a family room, and two bedrooms. One of these bedrooms ends in an acute angle at the back of the house to take advantage of a small view corridor to the city below. The architect explains, "An overarching goal is to make the lower level not feel like a basement; light from multiple directions achieves this. The basement courtyard is a primary feature of the house, with shadows reflected from a trellis above at certain times of the day, while the white marble water feature with water spilling down its face reflects light deep into the house." The main level includes a combined living and dining area, the kitchen, and an additional bedroom, as well as the master bedroom suite. Outdoors, the angled infinity pool projects toward the city and serves to screen out the view of the house below. The mass of the kitchen acts as a barrier between the street and helps to maintain the privacy of the garden. On the top level there is a rooftop deck with seating and dining areas that take full advantage of the views available to the city below. The yard is contained by the two wings of the house, which frame the view from the entry.

Opposite: Looking down at the water feature in the direction of the entry bridge.
Following double page: The interiors of the house are revealed from the bridge over the entry level.

Opposite: The primary areas of the house access the water feature with more formal spaces above and entertainment spaces below.
Following double page: A view across the pool from the master bedroom, looking toward the kitchen.

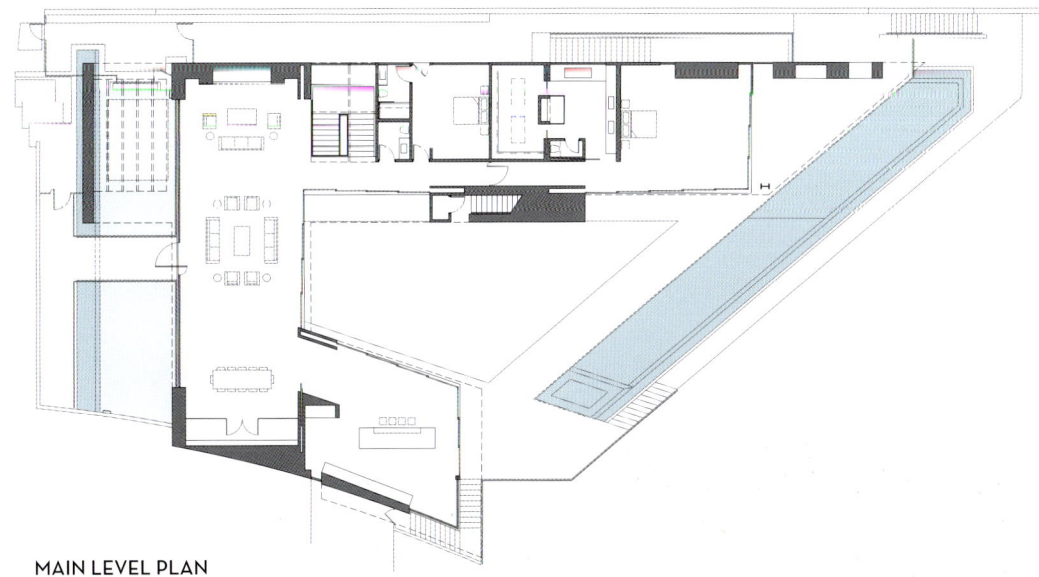

MAIN LEVEL PLAN

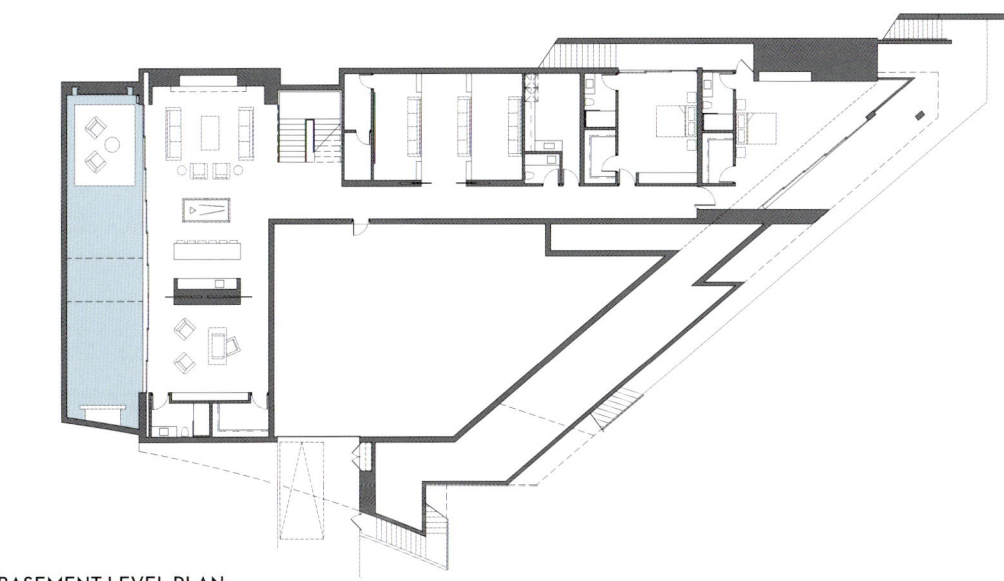

BASEMENT LEVEL PLAN

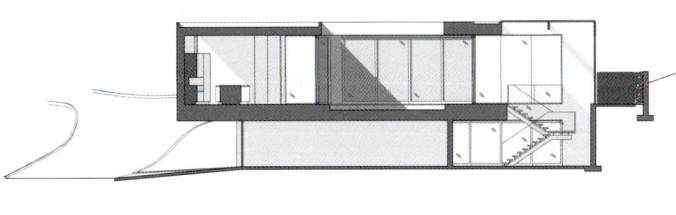

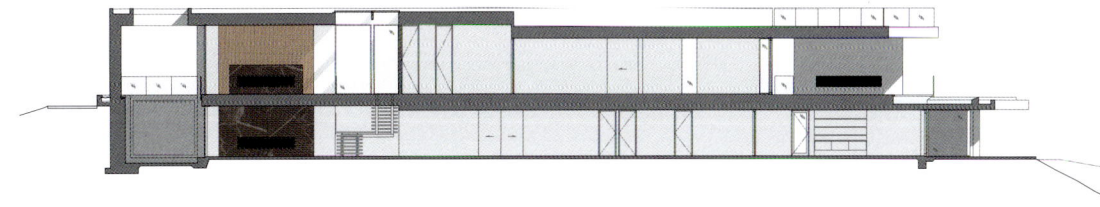

SECTIONS

WILLIAMS

Williams Lane is located near Carla Ridge in the Trousdale Estates area of Beverly Hills. The Williams Lane house was designed between November 2012 and May 2013 and completed in December 2015. This house was designed for the developer Nile Niami. The 25,246-square-foot lot allowed for a long entry driveway that makes the house visible only on entrance to the drive court. The main level houses the living and family rooms, a bar, and kitchen and dining spaces, as well as the master bedroom and two other bedrooms. A very large skylight over the dining room table allows for what the architect calls "dining under the stars." The architect states, "There was limited space for the program on the main level while still including a rear garden and pool. We made extensive use of sliding glass walls that disappear and connect the living spaces directly to the garden. The house appears perched above the city with stunning views from each of the main living areas. The infinity edge pool was pushed forward to shield views of the houses below and, along with hedges, ensures the privacy of the owners." A wide stairway leads down to the basement, which has the garage, a gym, a media room, a large beauty and spa area, and entertainment and wine rooms, as well as a bedroom and a water-feature courtyard. The water court contains an olive tree that adds a level of warmth and a sense of a garden. This house also incorporates a show garage at the lower level, which allows the owner to display an exotic car visible from the main entertaining areas.

Opposite: The dining room is dominated by a generous skylight.
Following double page: In this view across the living space toward the bar, the house appears to float above the landscape in the distance.

"THE SOFT WHITE HUES OF THIS HOUSE ENHANCE THE ENJOYMENT OF THE SURROUNDING VIEWS, WHILE THE LIGHTNESS AND BRIGHT TONES SPEAK TO ITS ELEVATED LOCATION."

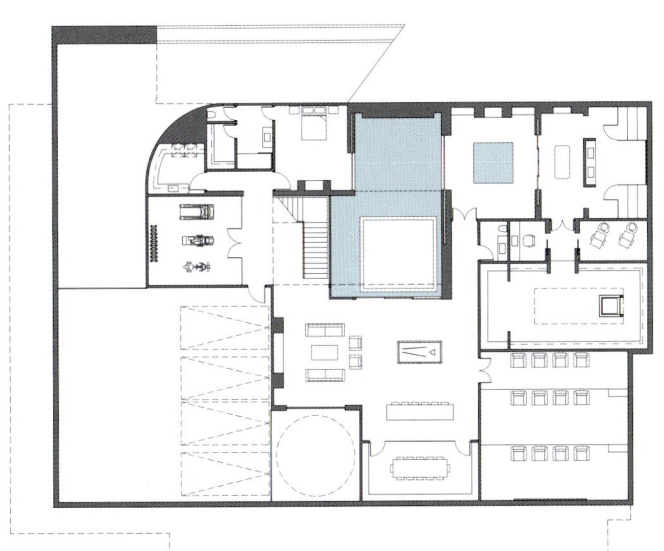

BASEMENT LEVEL PLAN

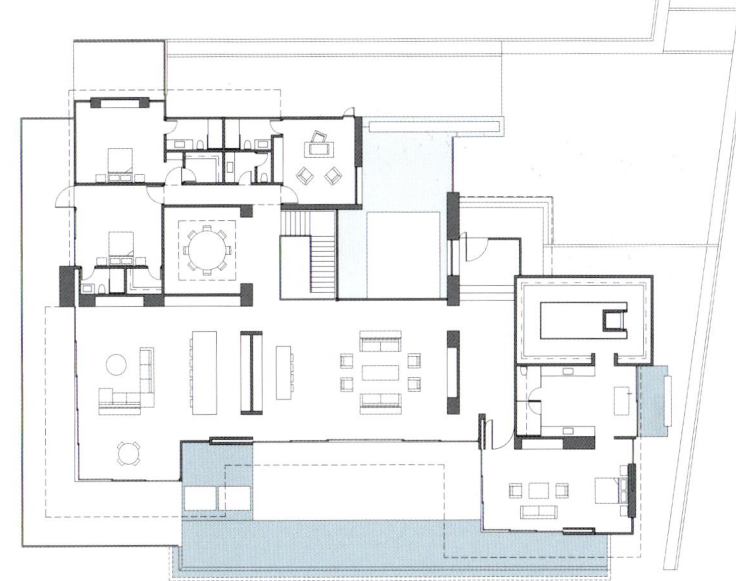

MAIN LEVEL PLAN

Opposite: A wide marble staircase descends to the entertainment level.
Following double page: At night the house comes alive with the upper levels focusing on the view and the lower levels looking into a water courtyard.

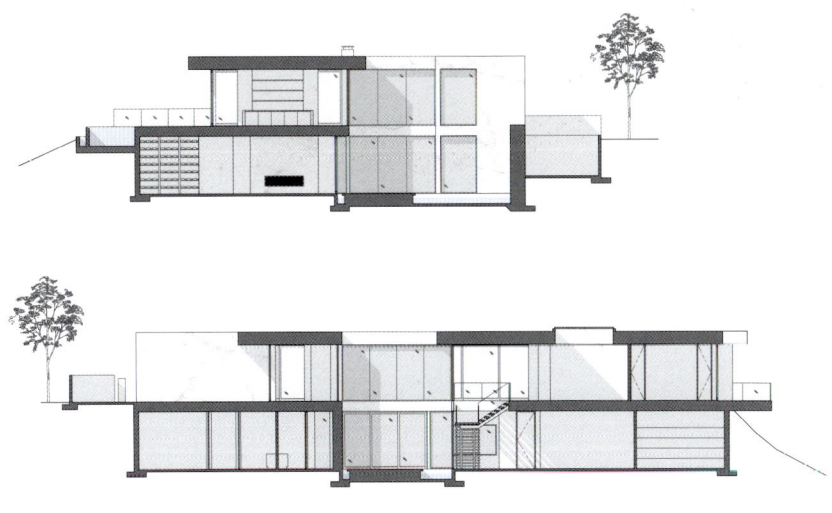

SECTIONS

DOHENY

Completed in January 2016, this two-story residence occupies a generous but steep and triangular 18,070-square-foot site. "Our concept," says Paul McClean, "was to push the hillside back as far as we could to create a buildable area and then figure out a way to reorient the home to face the view rather than the street." The solution was to put a water wall around the house to create an entry sequence that brings the view of the city into focus as guests and residents traverse a bridge and glimpse the living room. A twenty-foot double retaining wall covered with water wraps around the slope, creating the entry approach. The water cascades into the basement courtyard. In many of his plans, the architect uses curves or circles in the entry courtyard and in some cases the pool, but here the form of the site requires a broad curve that includes the dining area on the main level and the neighboring infinity pool. The other forms of the house are essentially rectilinear. The basement level has an area of 4,985 square feet, and is the location of the 564-square-foot garage, the entertainment and family areas, a bedroom, and a gym. The 4,050-square-foot main level thus has the master bedroom, which opens toward the pool, the living and dining area, and a kitchen finished in Stellar White marble that bridges over the water feature below. This space has wall-to-wall skylights and floor-to-ceiling glass on both sides, "enhancing the feeling of floating," according to the firm. Interior walls of the house are in Solto White and Stormy Sky marble. An unusual feature of the house is a 120-foot-long lap pool that runs along the entire southern side of the site. The main level is more focused on the view than the basement level is, as the latter, the architect says, "contains more intimate spaces wrapped around the water courtyard." With an emphasis on its steel frame and large glass surfaces, the house projects in the direction of the infinity pool and out to the view of the city beyond. Exterior walls are in Hudson limestone. In the architect's words, "This house is all about creating a sequence of spaces that maximize their connection to the view and the city while making the most of a tight lot configuration." The house was the first home that McClean did in collaboration with developers Cody Leibel and James Curnin.

Opposite: View of the pool that runs the length of the lot, near the master bedroom.
Following double page: As visitors walk on the entry bridge along the curving water wall, the view is slowly revealed.

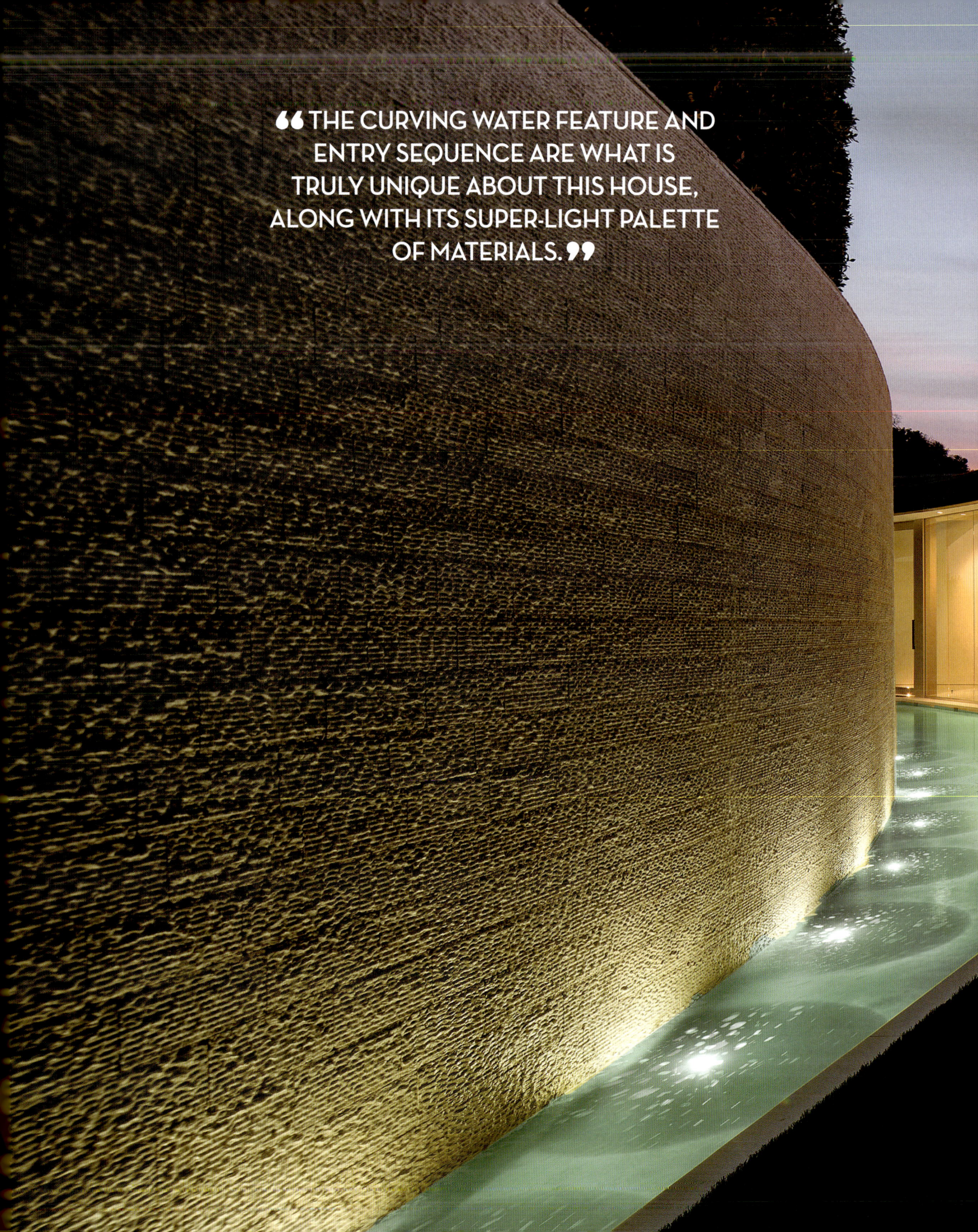

"THE CURVING WATER FEATURE AND ENTRY SEQUENCE ARE WHAT IS TRULY UNIQUE ABOUT THIS HOUSE, ALONG WITH ITS SUPER-LIGHT PALETTE OF MATERIALS."

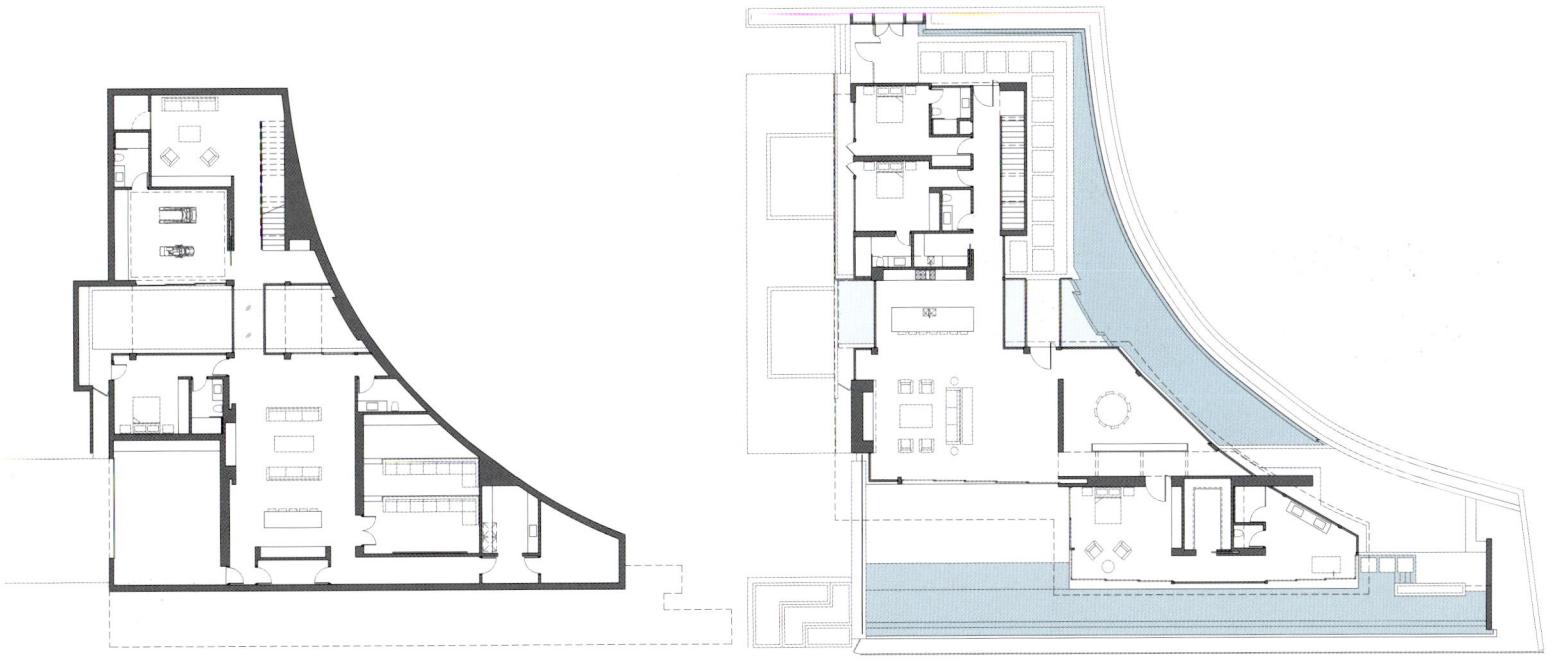

BASEMENT LEVEL PLAN

MAIN LEVEL PLAN

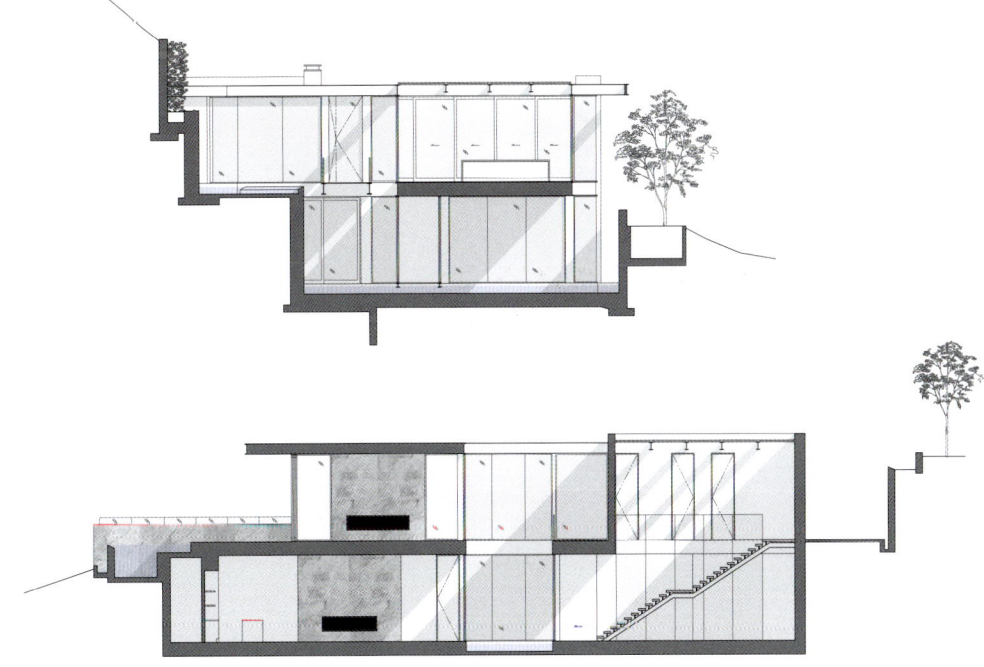

SECTIONS

Opposite: The primary rooms on the main level all connect directly to the pool and terrace.
Following double page: Views of the basement and the water feature that drops down from above. At right, the glass wine cellar provides visual privacy between the dining room and the master bedroom.

HILLCREST

Hillcrest Road is to the west of the Bird Streets, in the southern part of the Trousdale Estates area of Beverly Hills. This house was completed on a 26,865-square-foot lot in August 2016. Zoning regulations in the area impose a fourteen-foot height limit and do not allow basements to open to daylight and also restrict development of the pad area. The design shields the house from the busy street with a gated drive court that leads to a walled garden, a glass bridge, and a view of the pool and the city beyond the living area. The architect explains that this design "helps make the occupants aware, both physically and mentally, that they are leaving the world behind and entering a serene and calm space." A water courtyard at the basement level is the only source of natural light for the basement. In the basement, a theater and a wine cellar are located at the extremities of the floor plan, allowing the family room and gym to take advantage of the available light. To the rear of the house "roofs that hover over each other at different levels" reference mid-twentieth-century houses in the Trousdale Estates area, which were essentially single-story structures. Developed by Paul Trousdale (1915–1990), originally composed of 532 lots, the area includes houses owned by Elvis Presley, Frank Sinatra, Dean Martin, and Ray Charles. Living, kitchen, and dining spaces in the Hillcrest Road house are all on the main level, as is the master bedroom on the southwestern corner of the house. A terrace opens to the south from the living/dining area with views toward Century City beyond the pool. Three other bedrooms in the northwestern corner of the plan make up other private space for the residents. A warm material palette is made up of wood, split faced limestone, and dark brown marble, chosen to contrast with the light glass floor.

Opposite: Looking across the glass bridge to the garden beyond.
Following double page: As one steps through the garden gate, the house is revealed with its transparent living spaces framed by the stone walls.

“ THE CLARITY OF THE FLOOR PLAN WRAPPING AROUND THE WATER FEATURE, ALONG WITH THE CONTRAST BETWEEN THE TEXTURED STONE WALLS AND THE TRANSPARENCY OF THE GLASS, MAKE THIS HOUSE STAND OUT. ”

BASEMENT LEVEL PLAN

MAIN LEVEL PLAN

SECTIONS

Opposite: The two primary living spaces contrast in their outlook, with the basement level looking out to the intimate water feature, while the main level space has views of the city beyond.

The primary living spaces all open to the pool area. Privacy for the master bedroom is provided by the fireplace wall that introduces a soft limestone surface to the pool terrace.

MARCHEETA

Marcheeta Place is located just north of the Bird Streets in Los Angeles, in the hills above Sunset Plaza and is the second home in this volume designed for Cody Leibel and James Curnin. This house, built on a 13,380-square-foot lot, was completed in August 2016. In order to ensure the privacy of the clients, the architect placed a full height marble wall between the front yard and the house itself. The space between the wall and the house was made into a water courtyard and the glazed wall of the kitchen opens entirely to the water. The kitchen also opens toward the dining area and the family room on the 4,522-square-foot main level, implying that it is the center of the house. Inside the residence, a continuous skylight runs from the front door through the entire length of the structure, extending into the master bedroom suite. Outdoors, the infinity pool participates in the effort to create privacy for the home by restricting visibility of the house immediately below; its water spills down to the lower garden level. Construction in the area is limited to one story, so, as the architect states, "The main design challenge was to make the lower level not feel like a basement." The sloped site allows the lower level bedrooms and entertainment area to access the garden directly and to receive natural light. The stairway connecting the main and basement levels also serves to bring light into the lower area of the house. The gym and wellness area are located below the pool and skylights set in the bottom of the water draw filtered natural light into the space. The home includes a large-scale theater and cigar lounge next to the main entertainment area. The lower level has a floor area of 3,738 square feet. Floors are in Paloma limestone and Manhattan marble with interior walls in Nilo limestone, gray basalt, and Calacatta Lincoln marble. Ceilings are in white oak and exterior walls in white Macaubus quartzite.

Opposite: View of the water courtyard from the entry court that frames the view.
Following double page: A marble privacy wall screens the house from the street, in turn allowing a high degree of transparency on the view side.

"THE WARM PALETTE CONTRIBUTES HEAVILY TO THE ATTRACTIVE NATURE OF THIS HOUSE, WHILE THE FLOATING LIGHT-FILLED STAIRWELL CREATES A GREAT ENTRANCE TO THE LOWER LEVEL ENTERTAINING SPACES."

Opposite: All the primary rooms have retractable glass walls that allow residents to expand the living space to the terrace and garden beyond.

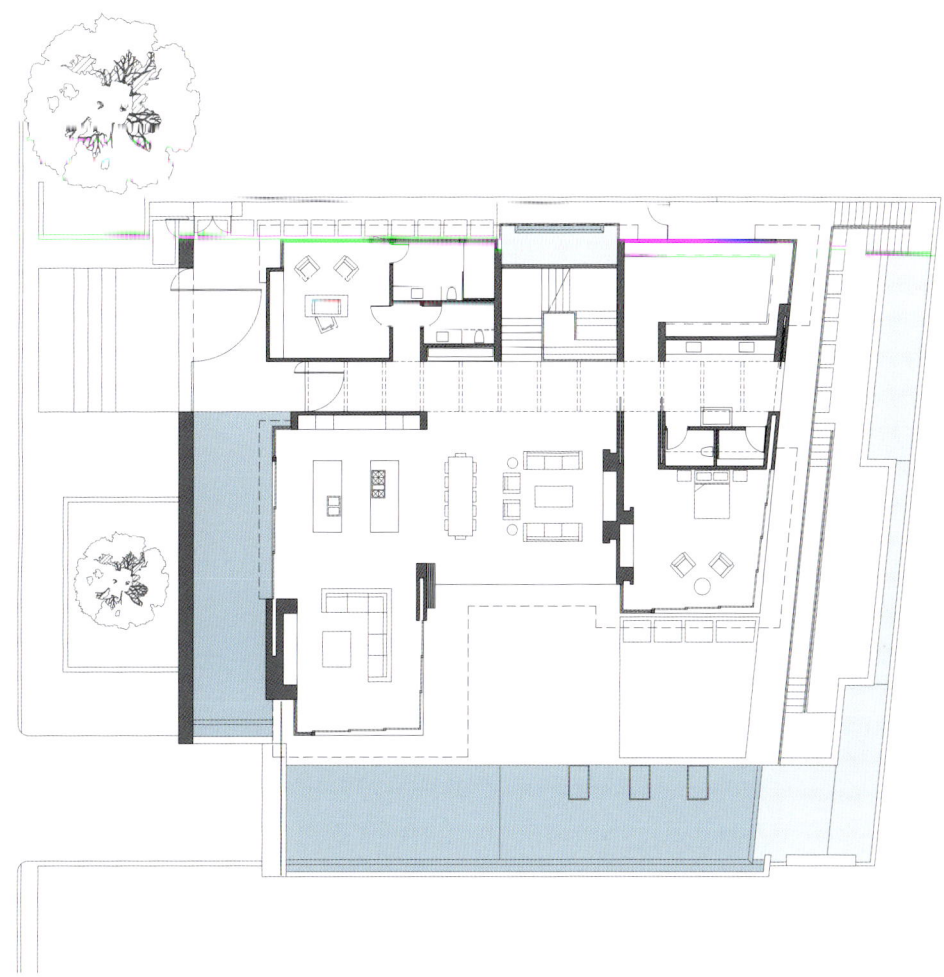

MAIN LEVEL PLAN

BASEMENT LEVEL PLAN

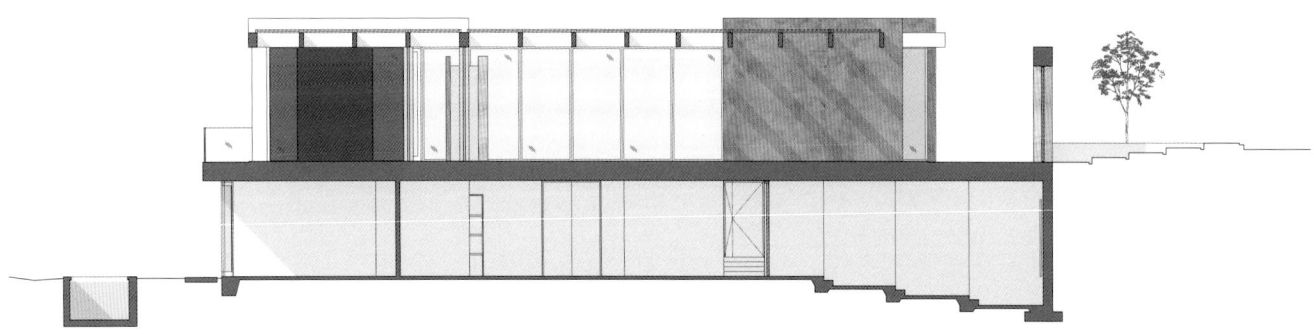

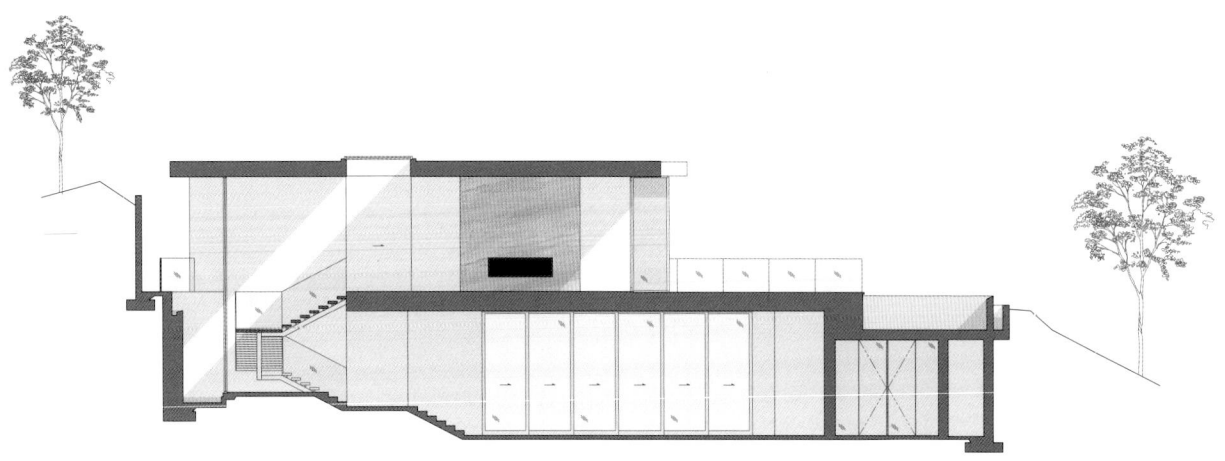

SECTIONS

Opposite: The kitchen opens directly to the water courtyard and the family area.
Following double page: A continuous skylight bisects the house from the entry to the master bathroom.

HILLCREST II

This house was designed for Nile Niami, who was closely involved in the material selection and programing of the home. Located, like the Hillcrest Road house in the Trousdale Estates area, this house occupies a 45,605-square-foot lot. It was completed in November 2016. The public and entertainment areas of the house all face the pool and a view of downtown Los Angeles, as well as the courtyard. Many of the private areas are in the northern part of the house, but all of the spaces have access to the central courtyard, which provides ample natural light. The architect explains that the central lap pool courtyard "is the key to the design." The house is entered by crossing a glazed foyer that spans a lower-level pool. This pool area allows the basement entertainment spaces and wellness area to receive natural light and is framed by a staircase at one end and a waterfall at the other. The master bedroom is on a split level due to site constraints, and the main living spaces are situated to take advantage of views over the infinity pool, while secondary bedrooms and an office benefit from an elevated setting above the street. Other amenities in this luxurious house include a large theater, a wine room with dining space, a champagne cellar, and several large entertainment areas. The house offers abundant natural light, two pools, and three water features in a palette of white and gold materials. A large underground garage permits the display of rare cars and motorcycles.

Opposite: The entry pavilion spans over the water courtyard below.
Following double page: The lower level pool as seen from the gym and wellness area.

"THE LOWER-LEVEL ENTERTAINMENT AREA IS THE MOST POPULAR SPACE IN THE HOUSE. THE FULL-SIZE LAP POOL BOUNCES AN AMAZING AMOUNT OF LIGHT INTO THE SPACE AND, COMBINED WITH THE PLEASANT SOUND OF THE WATERFALL, MAKES THIS A COOL AND WELCOMING SPACE."

MAIN LEVEL PLAN

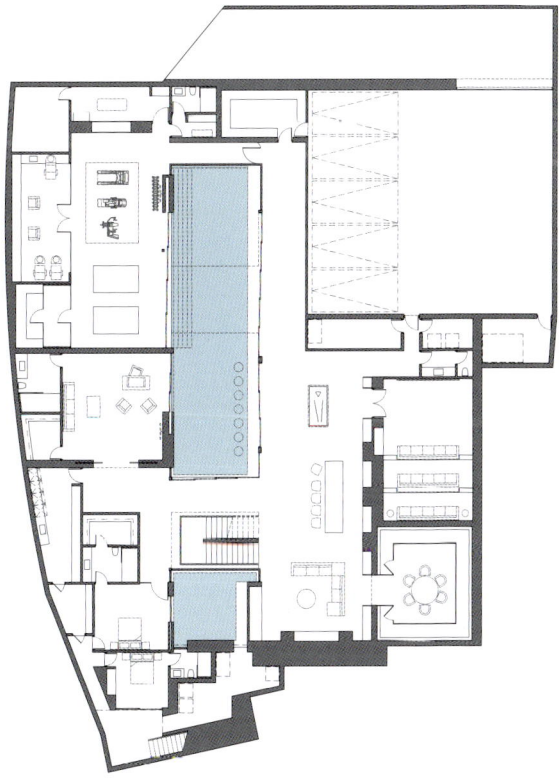

BASEMENT LEVEL PLAN

Opposite: The lower level entertainment space and wellness spa create a sense of luxury with light reflecting off of the central pool.
Following double page: The view side of the house incorporates a lounging area connecting into the pool.

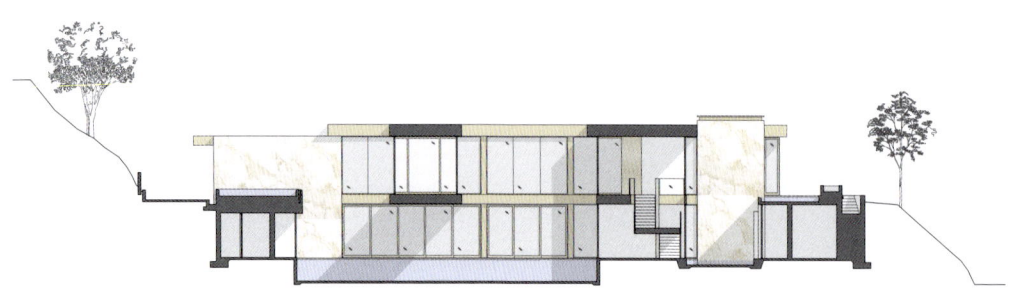

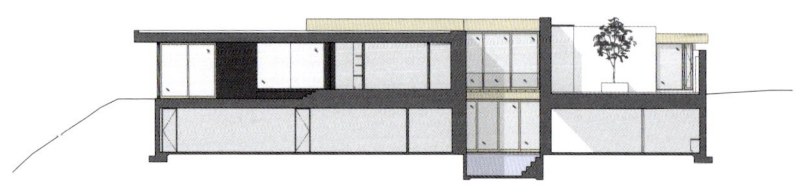

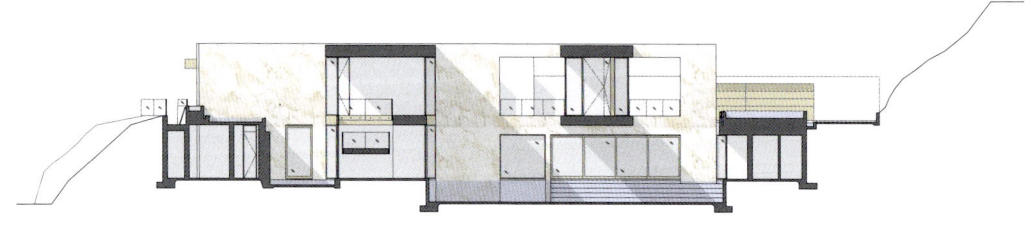

SECTIONS

BLUE JAY WAY III

Designed in 2014 and completed in June 2017, this house was built on a 10,864-square-foot lot and is the third house Paul McClean designed for developer Cody Leibel. The house has a 4,380-square-foot basement that includes three bedrooms and media and family rooms, as well as a four-car garage. The 3,804-square-foot main level has the master bedroom, a smaller bedroom, an office, and the kitchen/living/dining space. Outdoors on the same level is an infinity edge pool that plunges to a lower pool to the south, facing views of the city and beyond that the ocean. A large skylight over a floating stairway filters natural light to the basement, complementing the water courtyard and rear yard garden. According to McClean, "A continuous flat roof separated from the exterior walls gives the house a feeling of lightness, as light and warm wood ceilings seep from inside to out. The architect explains, "We wanted you to feel like you were floating over the city." McClean sought to give the residence a mid-century feel with light steel beams and low profile windows. Visible from the street, the house is built on a slope, which allows the lower level bedrooms to receive natural light from two sides and to open onto the back garden of the residence. Views are carefully edited and planting screen surrounding properties. The main materials employed for the exterior walls are Dolomite and Black River quartzite. Interior walls have the same cladding as well as drywall. Cabinetry is stained white oak and the floors are white terrazzo (main) and rift sawn oak planks (basement).

Opposite: Looking up from the lower level garden at dusk toward a water wall at the end of the garden.
Following double page: A view of the entry façade from the street emphasizes the floating nature of the roof.

> "FOR ME, THIS IS A QUINTESSENTIALLY CALIFORNIAN HOME, A STUDY IN BLACK AND WHITE WITH A VERY LIGHT TOUCH ON THE SITE, CONNECTING EPHEMERALLY TO ITS SURROUNDINGS."

MAIN LEVEL PLAN

BASEMENT LEVEL PLAN

SECTION

Opposite: The kitchen and living room share a common space that opens out to the garden and pool.

Opposite: At night with all the doors open to the pool terrace, the house is warm and inviting.

DEVLIN

Located east of the Bird Streets, Devlin Drive is north of the Sunset Strip. The owner of this project was McKillen Developments, based in Los Angeles and headed by Dean McKillen, son of Patrick "Paddy" McKillen, who is the owner of Château La Coste, near Aix-en-Provence in France. The house was designed from 2013 to 2014 and completed in November 2017. It has three levels and was built on a 48,078-square-foot lot. Exterior walls are in Sahara Noir marble, which is also used in the interior along with plaster. Floors are a combination of travertine, marble, and oak. The entry sequence of the house includes a water feature with an olive tree, intended to create a transition between the street and the entrance. Residents and visitors come into the house through a two-story space that immediately opens to a view of the city. The 5,660-square-foot main level includes the kitchen and family space, dining and living areas, office, media room, and a bedroom. The main spaces here offer access to the garden and terrace through a continuous, electronically-operated series of sliding glass doors. At this level, the pool cantilevers over the sloped site to expand the size of the garden and curves to match the contours of the property. The view over this infinity pool almost gives an impression of being in flight above the city directly below. According to the architects, "The continuous opening is the largest we have ever attempted and creates a situation where the entire lower level opens to the rear yard, connecting the house to the exterior environment." The 5,428-square-foot upper level has a family room, three smaller bedrooms, a gym, and a wellness center, as well as the master suite, which is in a cantilevered volume that appears to hover over the garden below. The smaller lower level where the motor court and garage are located has a staff bedroom. This is one of the few houses featured in this volume where the lot was large enough that the program did not require a basement.

Opposite: The master bedroom cantilevers over the terrace, creating a protected space that is out of the sun.
Following double page: Below the cantilever the entire glass front of the main level retracts into pockets to connect every room to the garden.

> "THERE ARE FEW SITES IN THIS PART OF THE CITY THAT ALLOW US TO EXPLORE A TWO-LEVEL HOUSE ABOVE GRADE, WHICH WAS ONE OF THE MOST REWARDING ASPECTS OF THIS DESIGN."

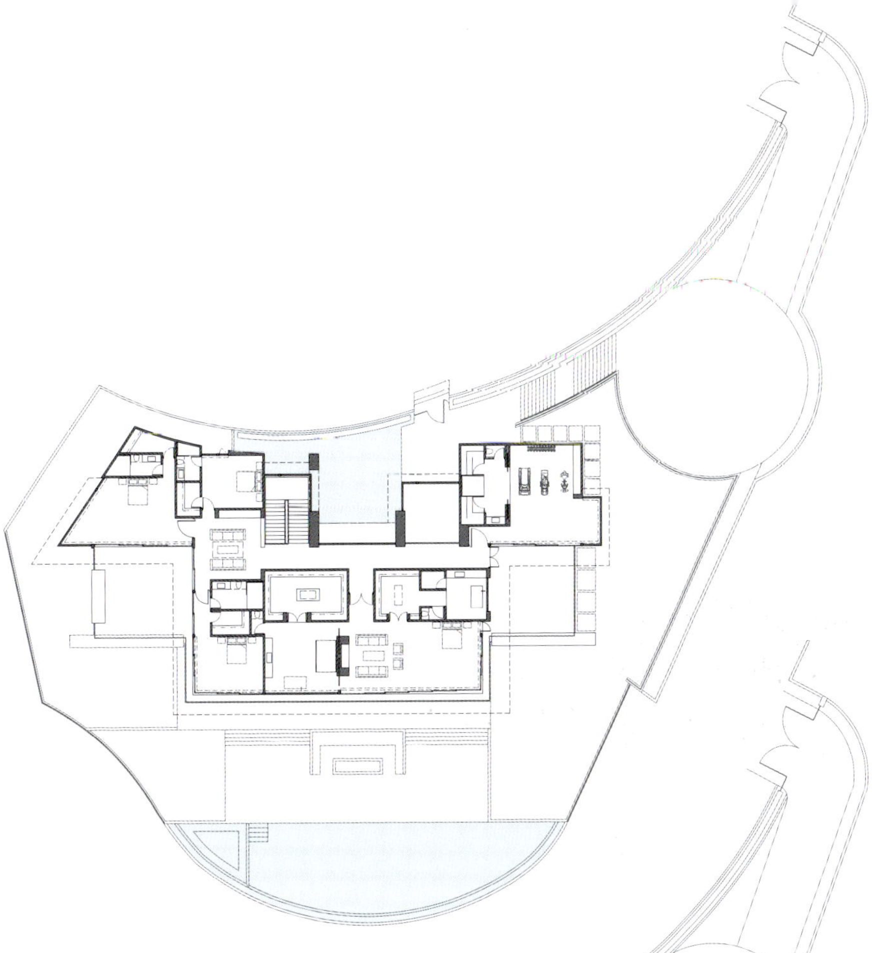

UPPER LEVEL PLAN

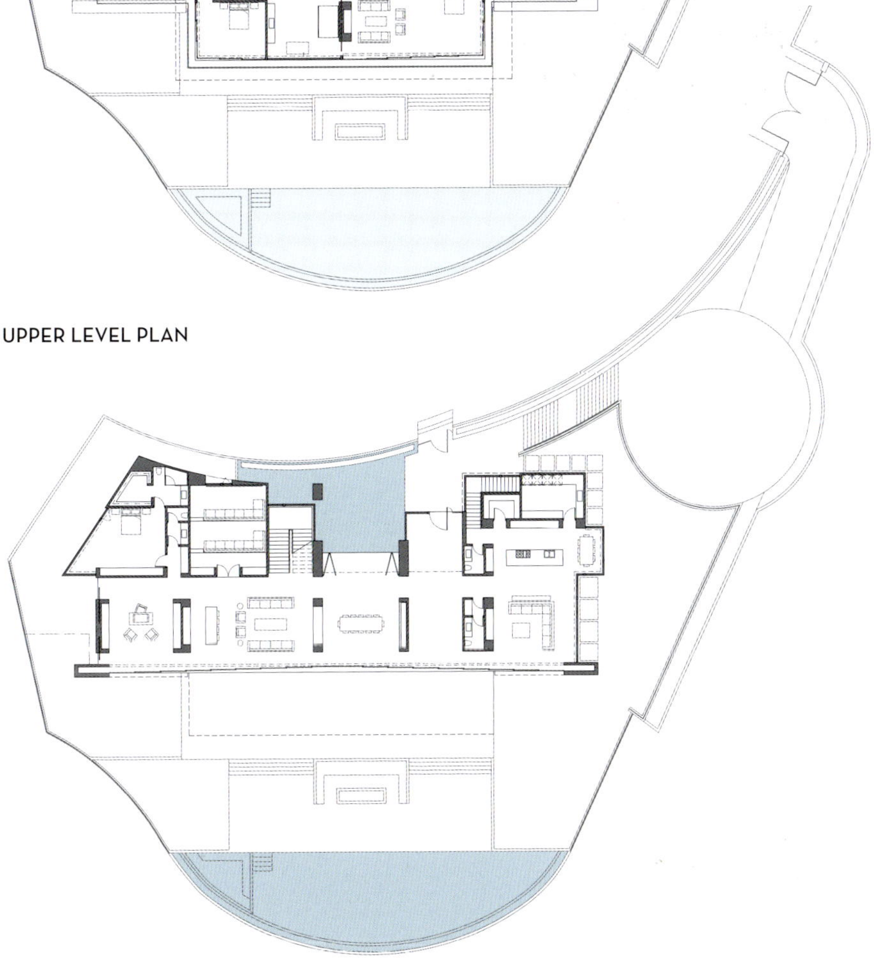

MAIN LEVEL PLAN

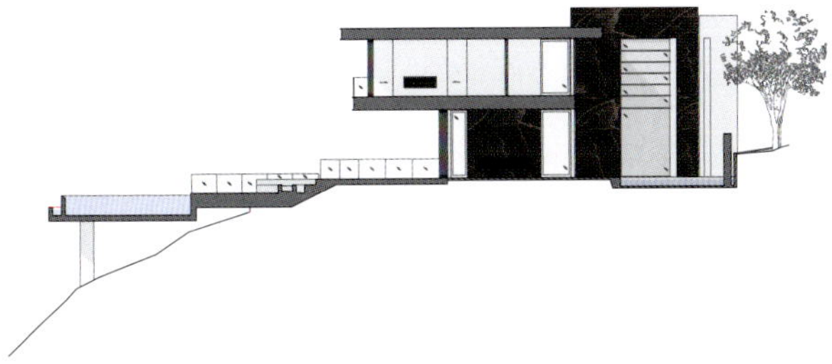

SECTION

Opposite: An olive tree appears to float in a water garden that brings light and air to the entry courtyard.

Preceding double page: The swimming pool screens the view of houses below, while the entry frames the more distant view.
Opposite: The house at night shows the living spaces spilling in a natural way out to the terrace and pool.

ROBIN

High above Sunset Boulevard, the Robin Drive house was built on a 28,033-square-foot lot in a fairly dense area with large homes located quite close to each other. The architect says that the biggest challenge of the project was "essentially how to fit a three-story house into a one-story community." The main level was dropped by eight feet to allow for the increase in floor area and keep the entire house within the required sixteen-foot height. The entry has a basalt rotunda that separates the house from the street and a two-story water wall spilling into a water garden, as well as an infinity-edge swimming pool facing spectacular views of the city. The form of the pool is generated by the site contours and the maximum height allowed above grade, and it is pushed to the extremities of the lot to increase the buildable area, as well as the garden spaces. The upper level is rotated ninety degrees as compared to the main floor in order to decrease visibility from the street and allowing the creation of a rooftop deck on the otherwise green roof. The master bedroom is cantilevered above the garden, creating a covered patio space below. The architect states, "The concept for living spaces is a glass pavilion with minimal walls, allowing a direct visual connection between the entry water garden and the pool beyond." The basement garage area includes a car display space, a bar, a golf simulation room, and a cigar patio. It also houses a media room, a lounge, a gym, staff quarters, and a kitchen, as well as a wellness area with a float tank and hydro-tub. Exteriors and interior walls of the house are in Bardiglio marble. Black basalt is also employed inside. Quartzite and oak as well as Palladio gray sandstone are also part of the interior material palette.

Opposite: The basalt entry rotunda as seen from the street, with the guest bedroom seeming to float above.
Following double page: The water garden as seen from the entry gate, with the living spaces appearing as a glass pavilion within the garden.

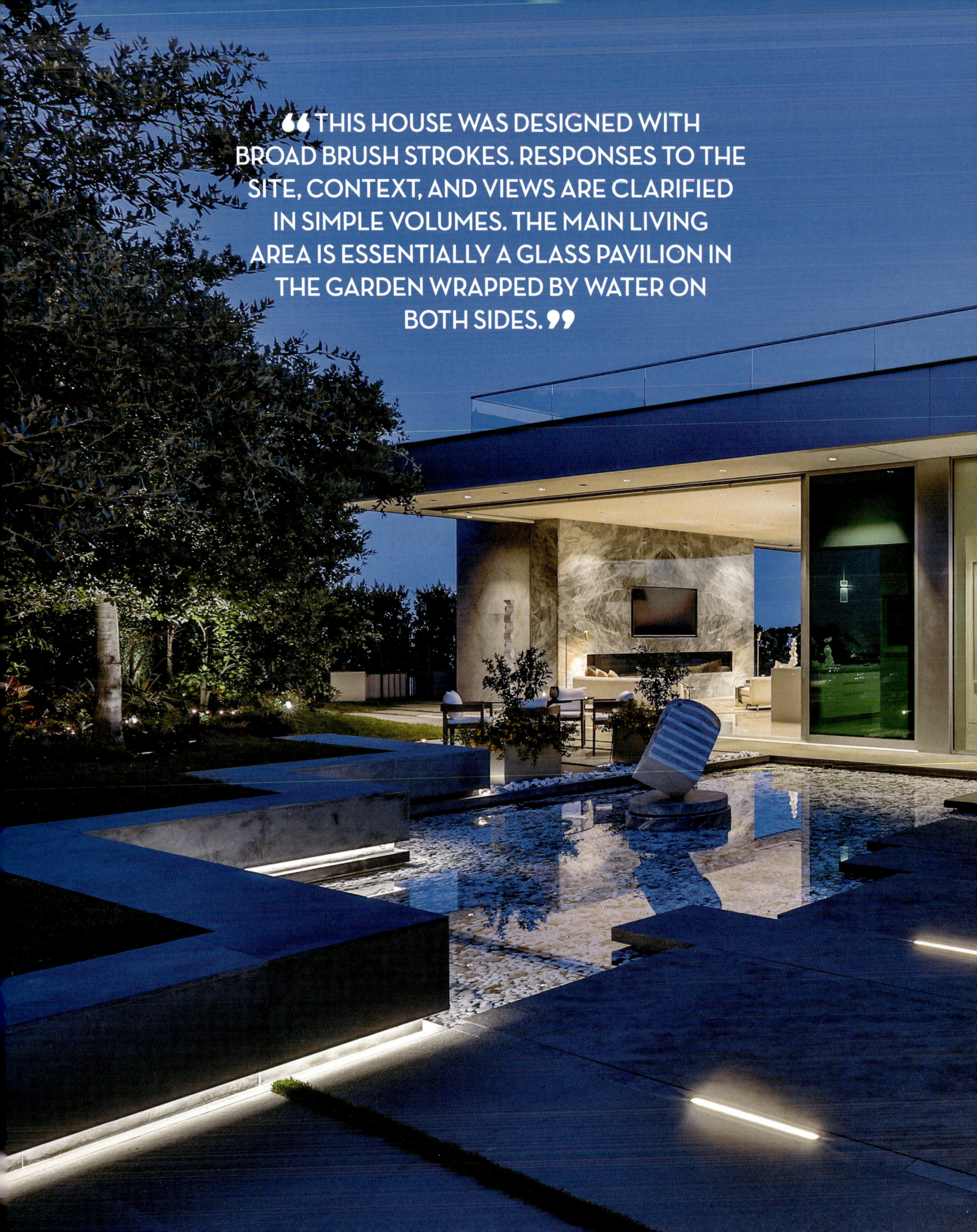

> "THIS HOUSE WAS DESIGNED WITH BROAD BRUSH STROKES. RESPONSES TO THE SITE, CONTEXT, AND VIEWS ARE CLARIFIED IN SIMPLE VOLUMES. THE MAIN LIVING AREA IS ESSENTIALLY A GLASS PAVILION IN THE GARDEN WRAPPED BY WATER ON BOTH SIDES."

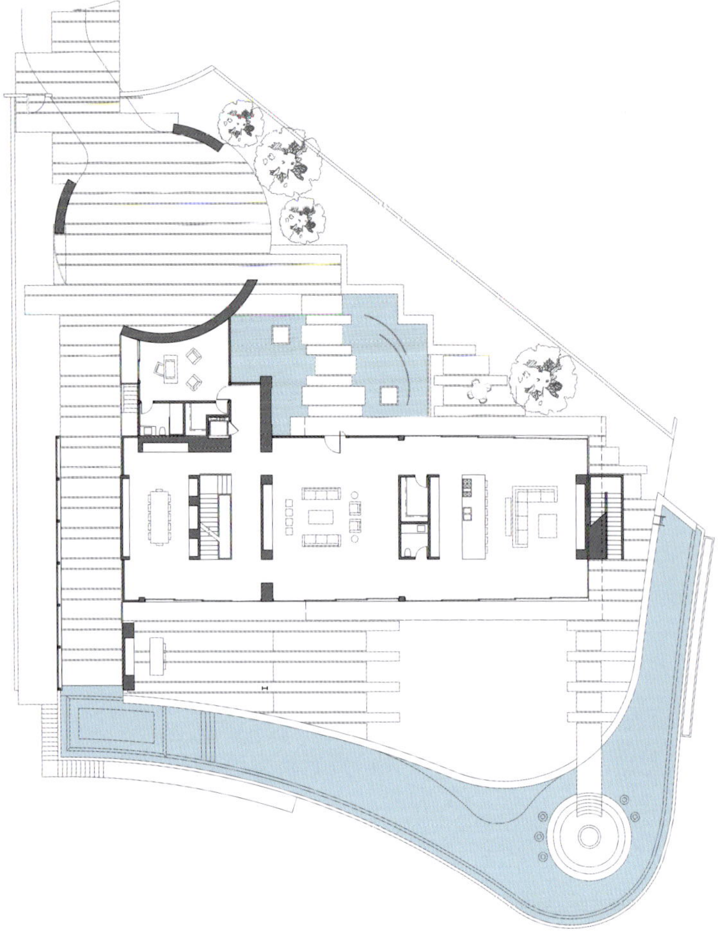

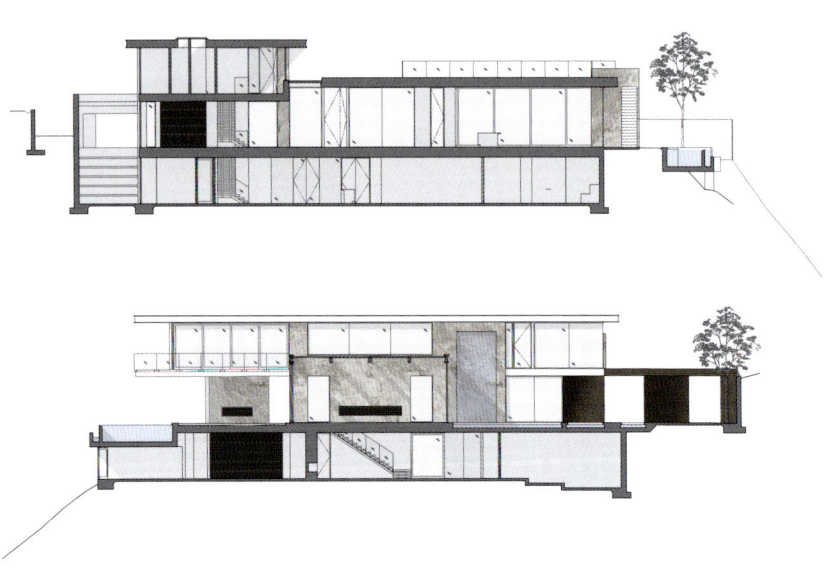

MAIN LEVEL PLAN

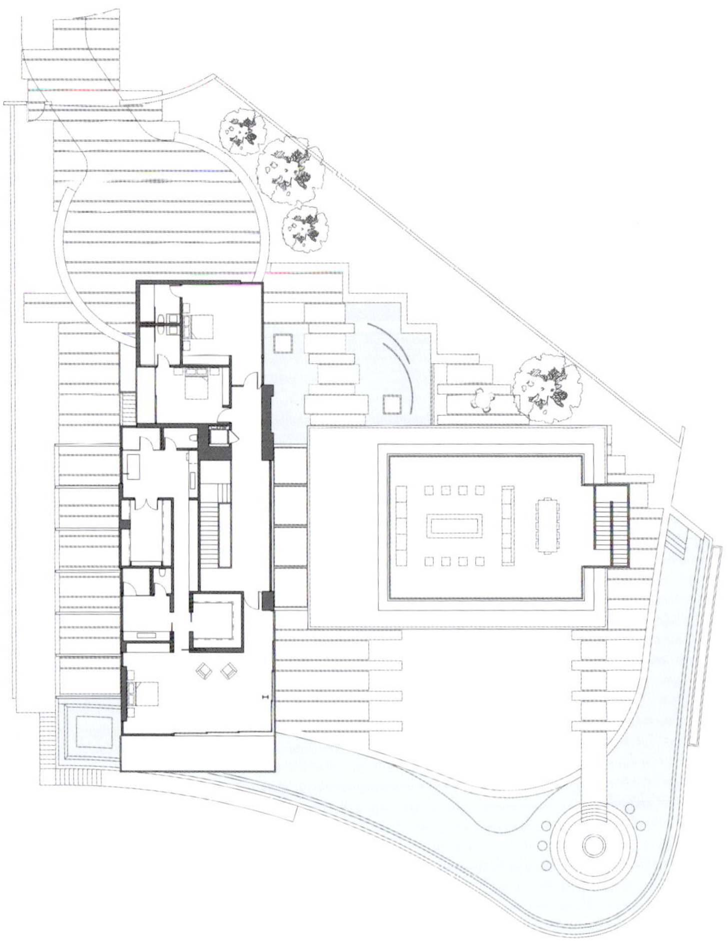

UPPER LEVEL PLAN

SECTIONS

Opposite: The pool terrace during the day and at night looking toward the master bedroom with the outdoor kitchen area below.
Following double page: The gardens on both sides rise above the family room and kitchen, providing views and privacy on both sides.

Previous double page: The curving pool is the signature design component of this house. It follows the lines of the site contours to wrap the entire garden.
Opposite: Looking back toward the house and garden from the circular firepit that is the focus of the pool.

SUNRIDGE

Located in Whistler, a resort town in British Columbia, seventy-eight miles north of Vancouver, this project represents McClean Design's first confrontation with a site subjected to severe winter weather. The 6,187-square-foot lot is steep and rocky. The architect states, "The house appears to be built into the rock hillside. It feels anchored and somewhat stoic. We love the contrast between the rugged cliff faces and rigor and clean lines of the architecture." The house, in fact, seems to sit rather firmly on real, solid mountain rock. Stone-clad exteriors and a warm interior palette "take cues from traditional ski chalets with the heavy use of wood throughout the home, but accomplished in a much more contemporary way." Set at the bottom of the ski slopes, the residence also provides for outdoor summer living with a swimming pool and spa. An exterior totem pole created by a local artist is inserted into a vertical niche outside the house. The three-level house has a two-car garage, a spa and gym, a family room, a media room, two bedrooms, and a kitchen on the basement level. The main floor has two more bedrooms, as well as the dining and living areas. On the upper level, the design provides for the master bedroom suite, as well as two additional smaller bedrooms. The number of bedrooms is consistent with the client's desire to host large gatherings of friends and family. The materials include basalt and Carrara marble contrasting with the extensive use of oak and walnut to create a "sheltered and warm feeling on snowy nights." While the building consists of refined materials, the exterior site walls were finished in rough stone "mimicking the mountainous landscape."

Opposite: A Native American totem pole commissioned from a local artist greets visitors at the entry to the home.
Following double page: View of the house from the driveway at street level, showing the house nestled into the rocky site.

“THIS HOUSE FEELS LIKE AN EXTENSION OF THE MOUNTAIN ITSELF AND HAS A UNIQUELY SOLID PRESENCE THAT FEELS GROUNDED IN ITS SURROUNDINGS.”

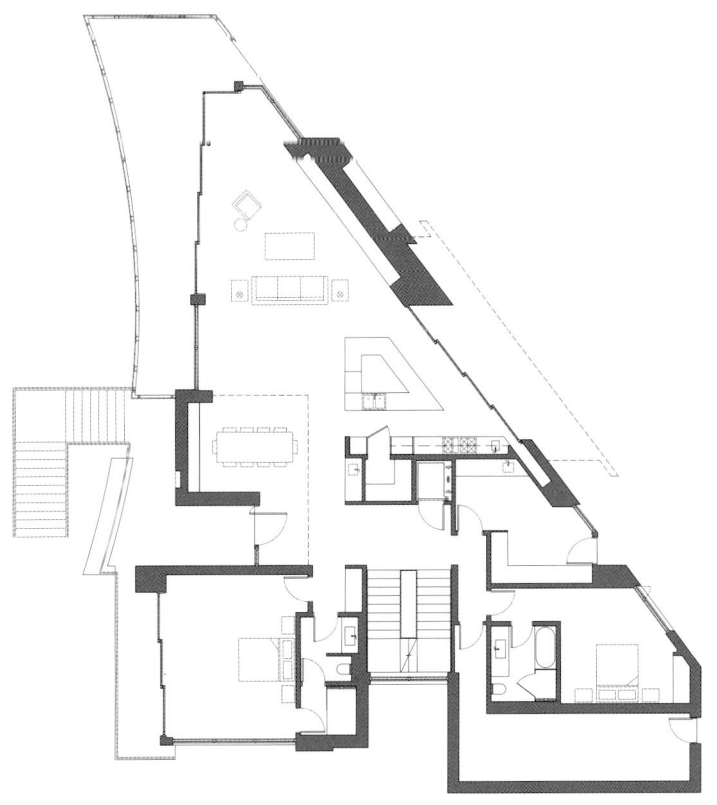

MAIN LEVEL PLAN

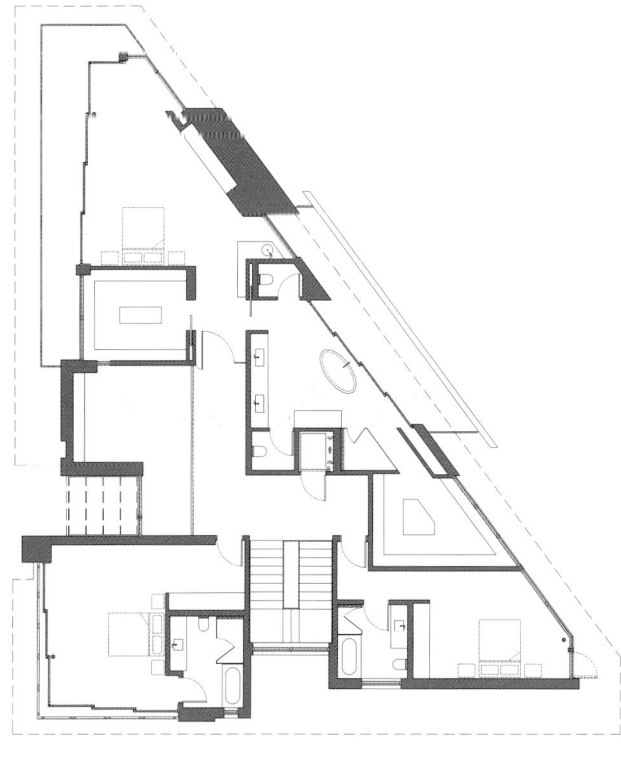

UPPER LEVEL PLAN

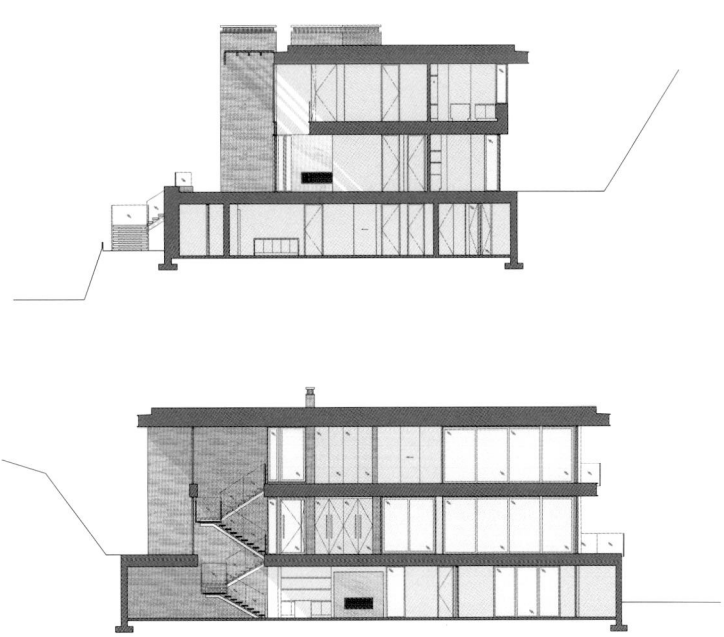

SECTIONS

Opposite: The living room and kitchen use a palette of materials that is warm and light, appropriate for the mountain environment

199

BEL AIR

This 30,000-square foot house was built adjacent to the street, on a large (51,417-square-foot) lot in the Westside area of Los Angeles. This precise location was chosen due to geological constraints and to allow for a large garden space to the rear. The main floor includes extensive terraces and a pool area that descends to a lawn terrace at the lower level of the three-story residence. The garden, partially set on a plinth-like structure, steps down in the direction of the city view. The entrance sequence, which serves to preserve the privacy of the owners by blocking the view from the street, begins with a lower level circular stone-walled motor court. A stairway leads up to the main areas of the house. A 180-foot-long water wall guides the visitor to the entry before dropping to a basement level water garden. Inside the house, a two-story hallway leads to the view and separates the formal living room and library from the dining room and family/kitchen area. Each room on the main level has access to a terrace and the view. The main level pool has an infinity edge that cascades down to the garden and the motor court. The lower level consists of additional bedrooms, a full wellness spa, theater, bar and entertainment spaces, and a ten-car garage. The upper level has a long north-south hallway that opens to the master bedroom and a balcony on the southeastern corner of the house, as well as three smaller bedrooms, two of which share a balcony at the northern part of the house. The roof deck includes a cabana, a fire pit seating area, and a bar. The architect paid careful attention to the scale of the spaces, maintaining a casual feeling despite the significant floor area of the residence. The extensive use of Caravela limestone, Moca Cream limestone, and oak was chosen to give the house a soft, contemporary look. Paul McClean says, "The way the house connects from the entry sequence to the outdoor entertaining areas, gardens, and views is one of the most successful parts of the project."

Opposite: The upper levels of the house appear to float above the water feature and stone rotunda wall.
Following double page: An evening view of the entire house reveals the transparency of the two upper levels.

"DESPITE ITS THREE LEVELS, THIS IS A VERY HORIZONTAL HOUSE, WRAPPED IN WATER AND LAYERED PLANTING TO SCREEN IT FROM SURROUNDING PROPERTIES AND KEEP THE FOCUS ON THE GARDEN AND VIEW."

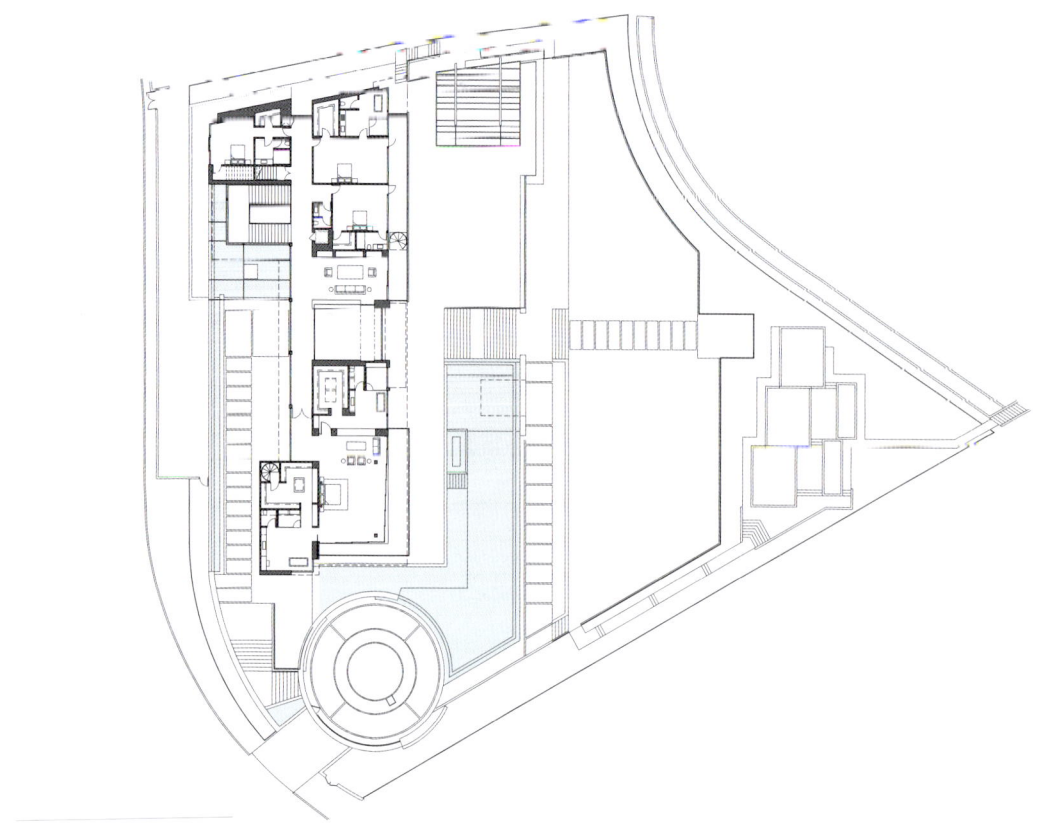

UPPER LEVEL PLAN

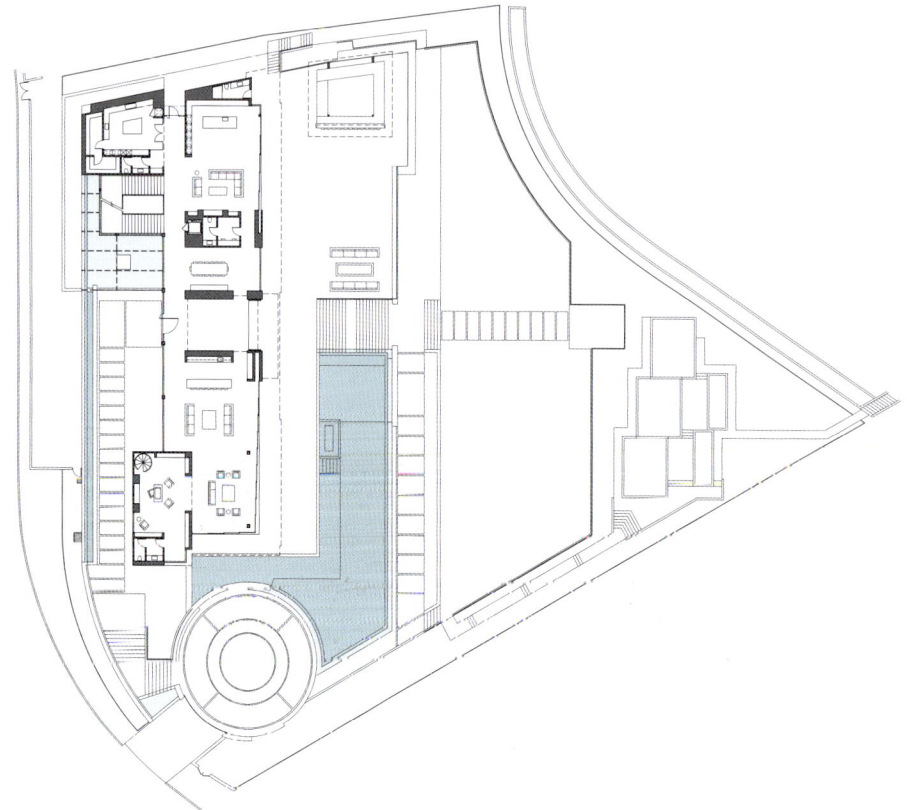

MAIN LEVEL PLAN

Opposite: The living and family rooms reveal a warm palette of limestone and soft wood as well as a direct connection to the expansive terrace.

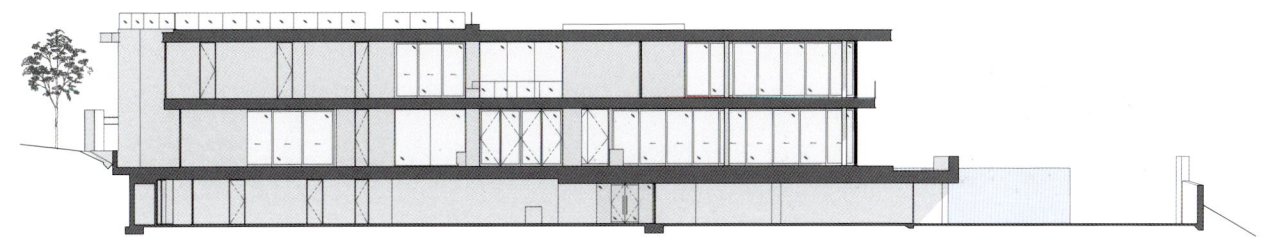
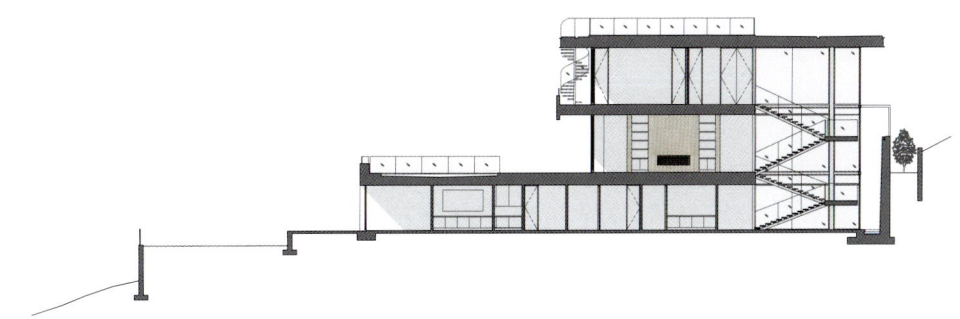
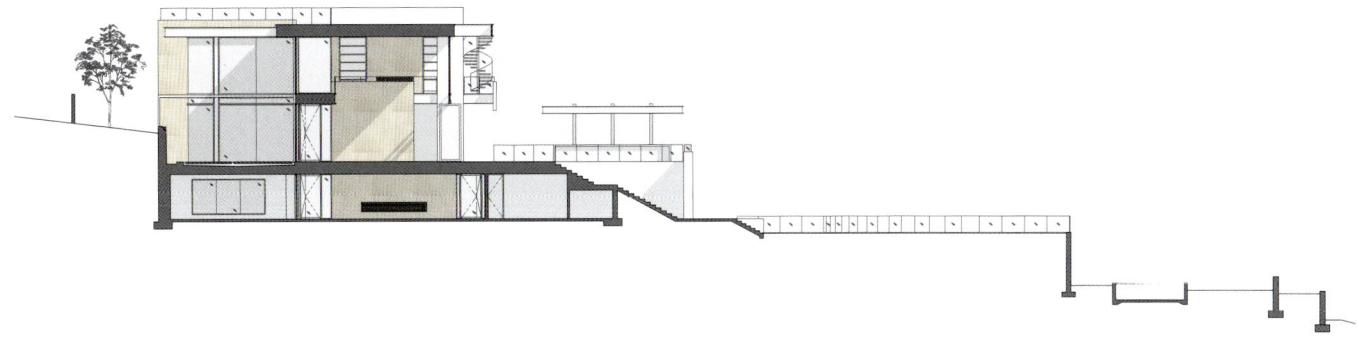

SECTIONS

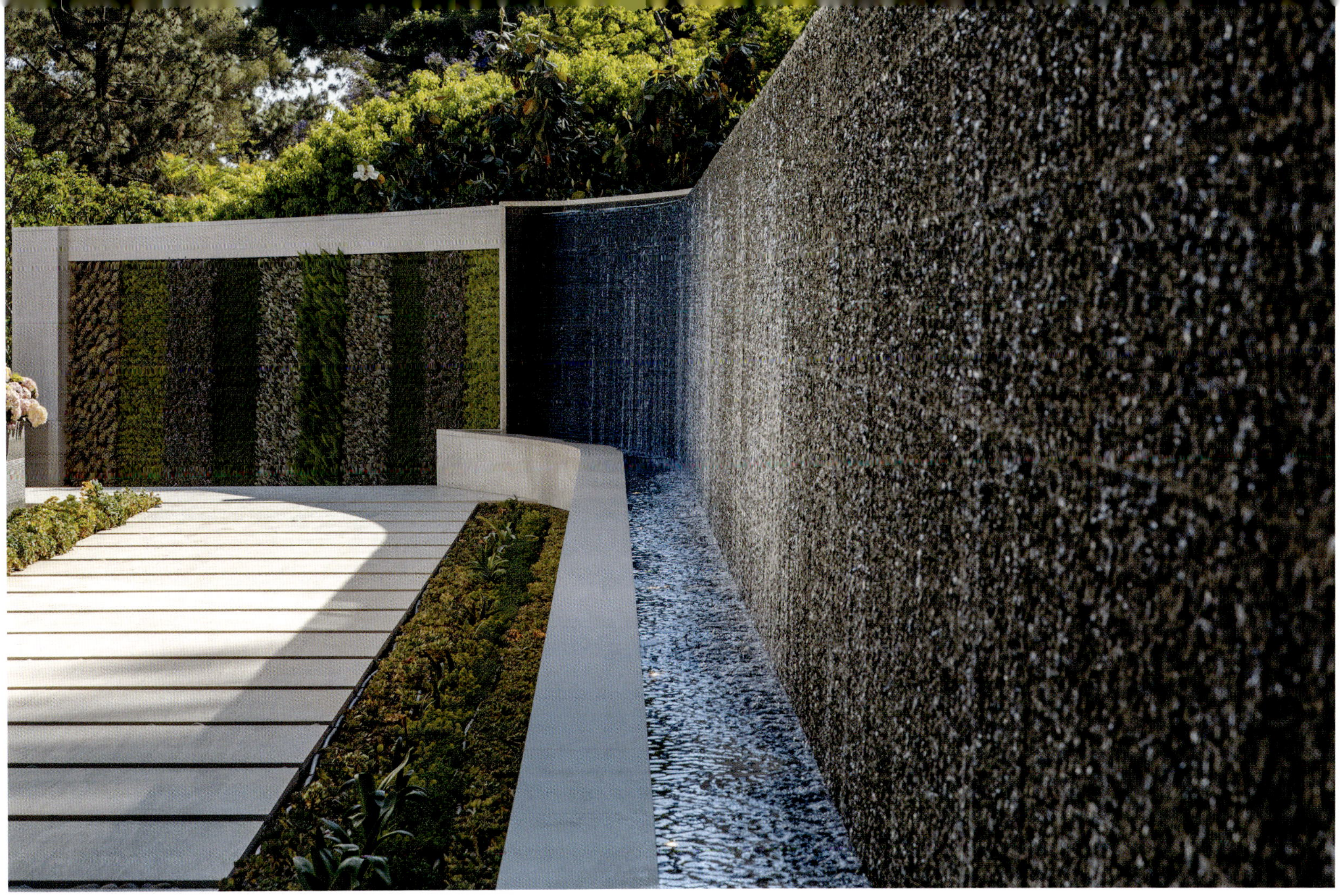

Opposite: A key component of the design is the entry garden with its walls of water and plants, connecting directly to the three-story glass stair.
Following double page: The house is seen mirrored in the large pool, with its ground-level spaces fully open to the exterior.

CARLA LANE

This two-level Beverly Hills house is located on a 24,451-square-foot site in the Trousdale Estates neighborhood with a relatively small buildable area. The house was designed for prominent interior designer Lindsay Chambers. The architect states, "The restrictive codes that we have been working under, plus our clients' aspirations for more programs and facilities, have moved us to use basements for the program and thus to look at different ways of transmitting light to the lower level." An entry courtyard is screened from the street. The garage is located on the lower level and reached by a ramp. It has a large window facing a sunken courtyard that contains a large rectangular water feature. A transparent entry bridge crosses over this courtyard, leading to the living area in the direction of the rear outdoor infinity pool with views of Century City. The kitchen and family room open to the rear garden, while the dining room is contained in a glass area that bridges over the courtyard. The triangular upper level pool has a shallow shelf that wraps around the master bedroom, in Paul McClean's words, "creating a feeling that this part of the house is floating on water." A spa (gym and sauna) and fireplace are on the garage level, as are a bar and family lounge. Generous operable glazing gives the house a feeling of lightness and openness that is surely appropriate to the Los Angeles climate. In fact, seen from the garden side, the house appears to be made up of a narrow black roof plane sitting above the pool, with its walls largely made of glass, with only relatively thin black columns connecting the roof to the ground level. This is in direct contrast to the street side of the home, which is predominantly clad in limestone bricks, giving only fleeting glimpses to the interior through a bronze lattice screen. Furnishing and finishes are soft and modern, with an emphasis on the white to beige color range.

Opposite: The entrance path to the house offers a view to the garden on the opposite side.
Following double page: On entry, the visitor perceives a solid stone courtyard that gives way to a glass bridge over water leading to the transparent living space.

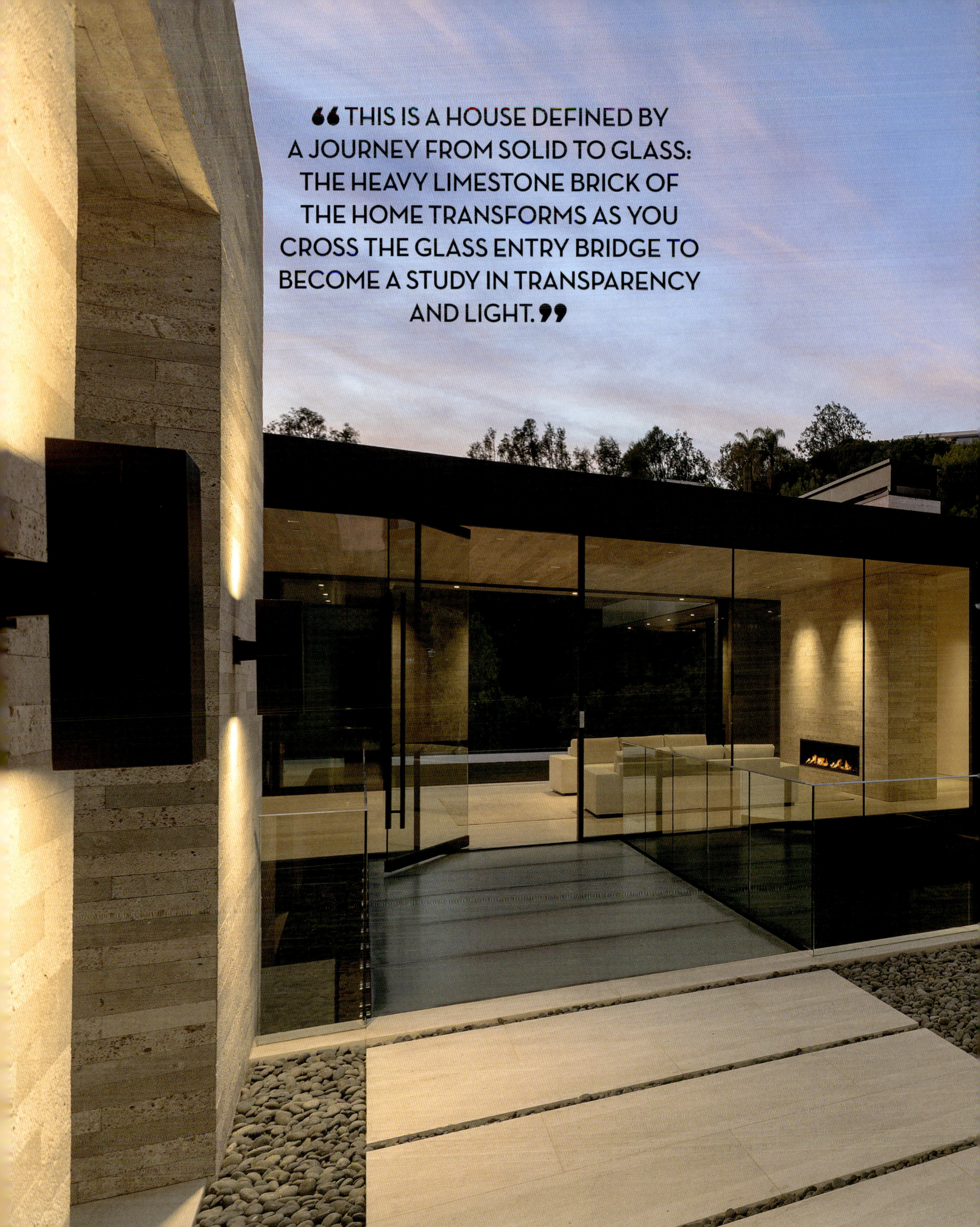

"THIS IS A HOUSE DEFINED BY A JOURNEY FROM SOLID TO GLASS: THE HEAVY LIMESTONE BRICK OF THE HOME TRANSFORMS AS YOU CROSS THE GLASS ENTRY BRIDGE TO BECOME A STUDY IN TRANSPARENCY AND LIGHT."

MAIN LEVEL PLAN

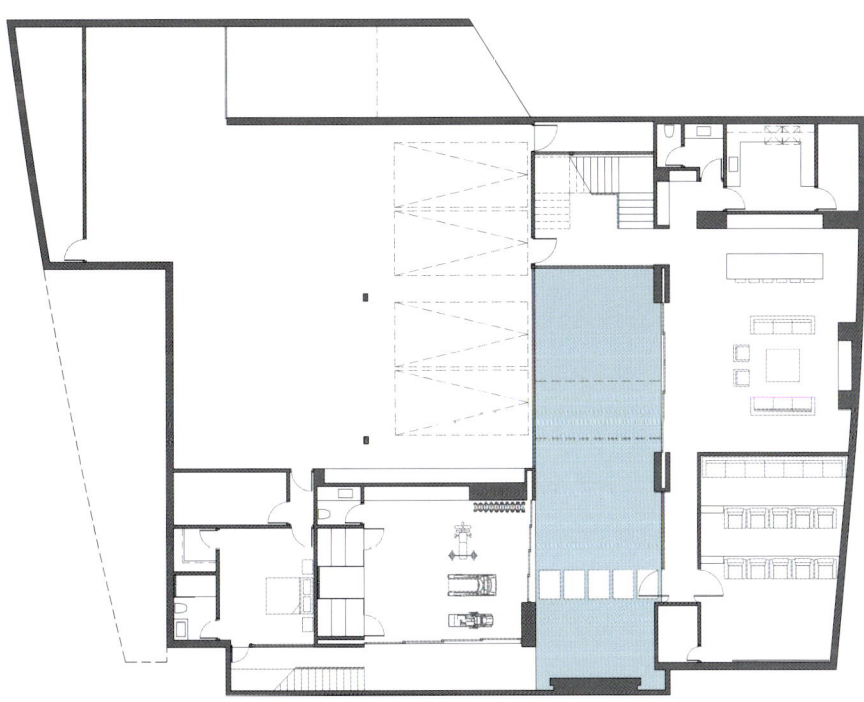

BASEMENT LEVEL PLAN

Opposite: The kitchen opens fully to the rear garden through the family room. The living space reveals a soft palette of limestone and wood.

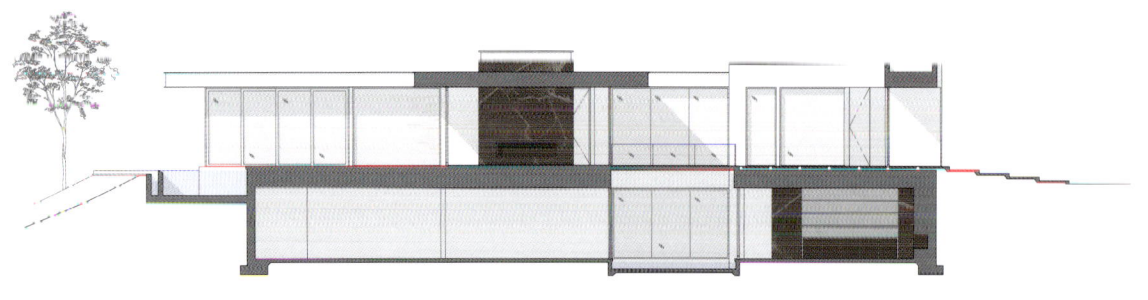
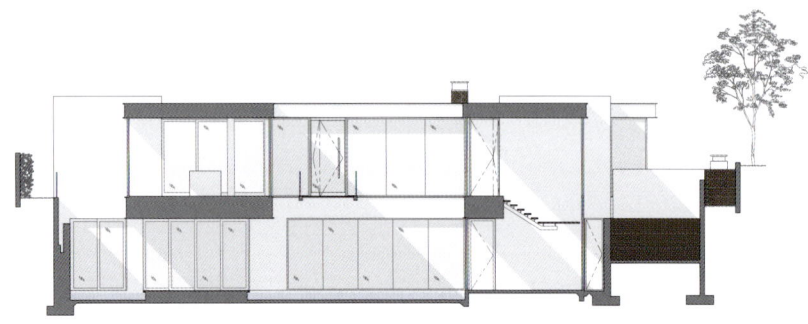

SECTIONS

Opposite: The lower level entertainment area opens directly to the water garden.
Below: Looking back across the glass entry bridge.
Following double page: Looking in the direction of the family room from the master bedroom area, the house is reflected in the pool at sunset.

SKYLARK

Located in West Hollywood on Skylark Lane, this house was built on a steep 30,744-square-foot lot at the end of a narrow private street. The first impression that visitors have of the house is one of openness, with the second level appearing to float over the entry terrace and parking area, revealing views toward the ocean and the west side of Los Angeles. In place of a conventional garage the house has two elevators that transport cars to the basement. Entry to the house is via a bridge over a three-level light well. A water wall cascades to the court below, which divides the basement in two. At the upper level two additional bridge components link the bedrooms to the two-story living room and loft. These spaces are the focal point of the house and have large tilting glass walls that lift up to become canopies over the terrace. These glass walls make the inside and outside decks of the house into a continuous living space. The architect explains that the house "has a somewhat industrial feel, exposed wide flange steel columns and fascia detailing, for example." There are five bedrooms, living and family spaces, a gym, a media room, and two offices. The main level of the house, which is about half the size of the basement or the upper floor, houses the living, dining, and kitchen areas together with large terraces. The bedrooms, including a master bedroom suite, are located on the upper level. Exterior walls are in gray basalt, while Visconte, and Calacatta Gold marble and Absolute Black Zimbabwe granite are used for interior walls. Floors are in Caliza Gris limestone.

Following double page: A late afternoon view of the pool, which is open to the living and kitchen areas.

"THIS HOUSE IS ALL ABOUT MOVEMENT, WITH THE ELEMENTS OF THE PROGRAM PULLED APART TO EXPLORE THE SPACES AND VIEWS FOUND IN BETWEEN. THE CONSTRICTED SITE ENTRANCE AND LACK OF SPACE FOR AN ENTRY LED TO THE UNUSUAL SOLUTION OF PLACING MOST OF THE PROGRAM ABOVE AND BELOW THE GROUND PLANE."

Opposite: Very large tilting glass walls allow a direct connection between the great room and the pool and garden.

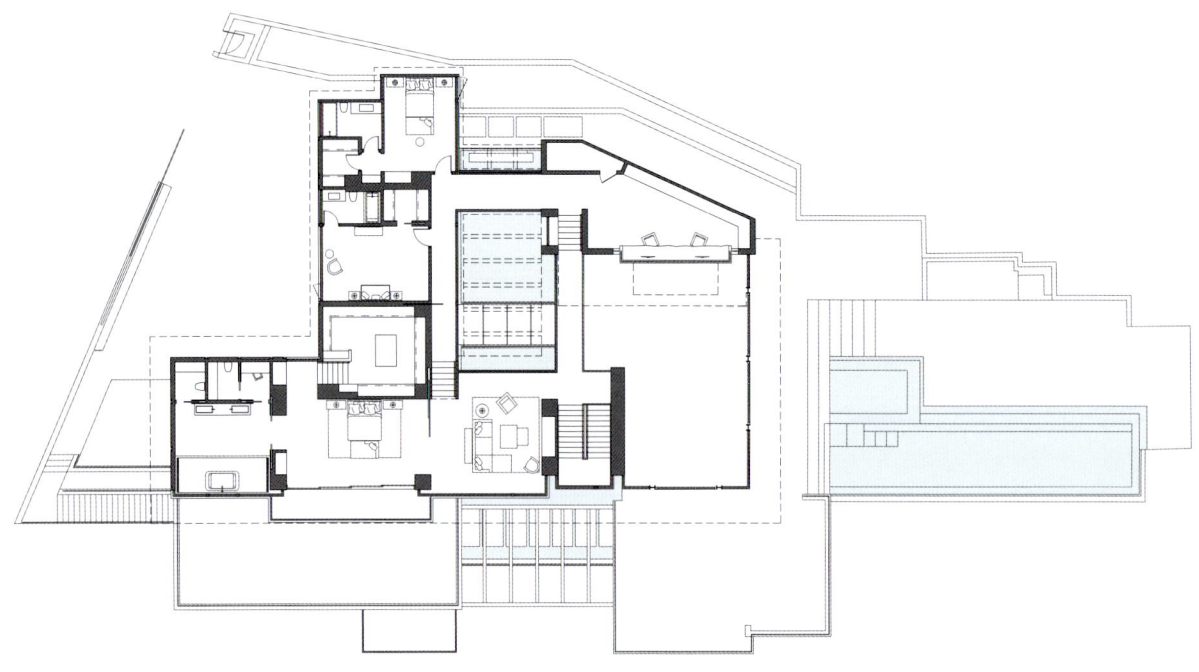

UPPER LEVEL PLAN

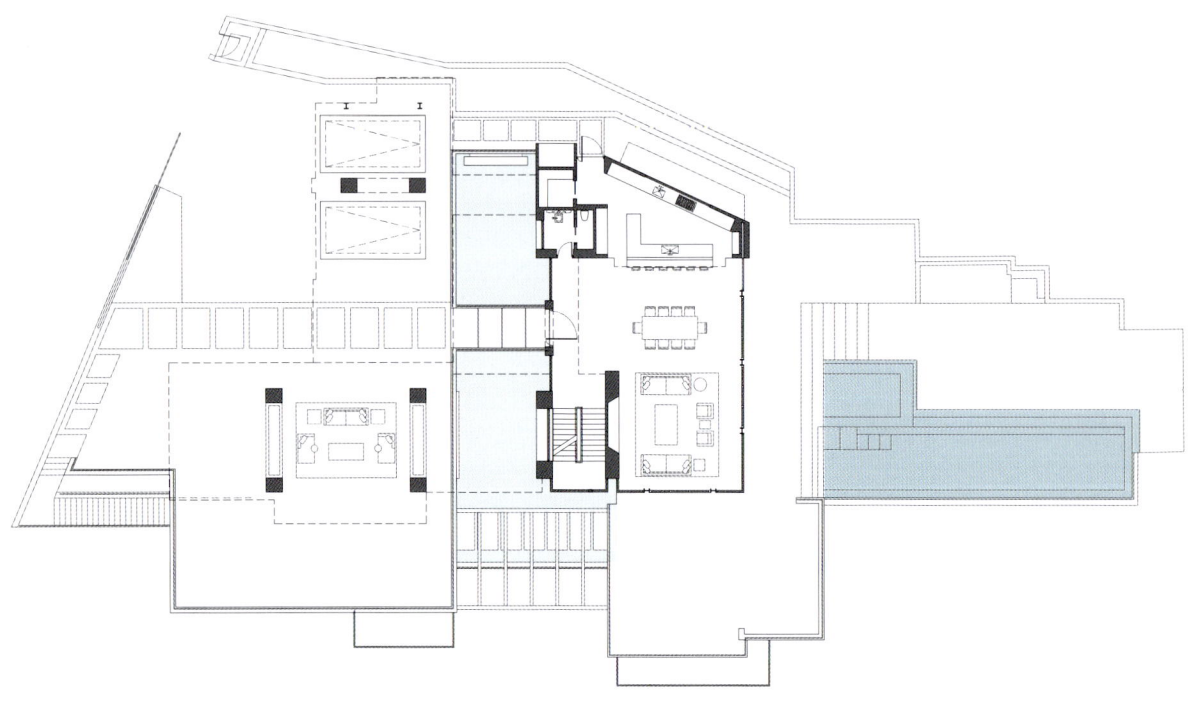

MAIN LEVEL PLAN

229

Opposite: The house is split by the three-story water courtyard with bridges and glazed hallways connecting the different levels.

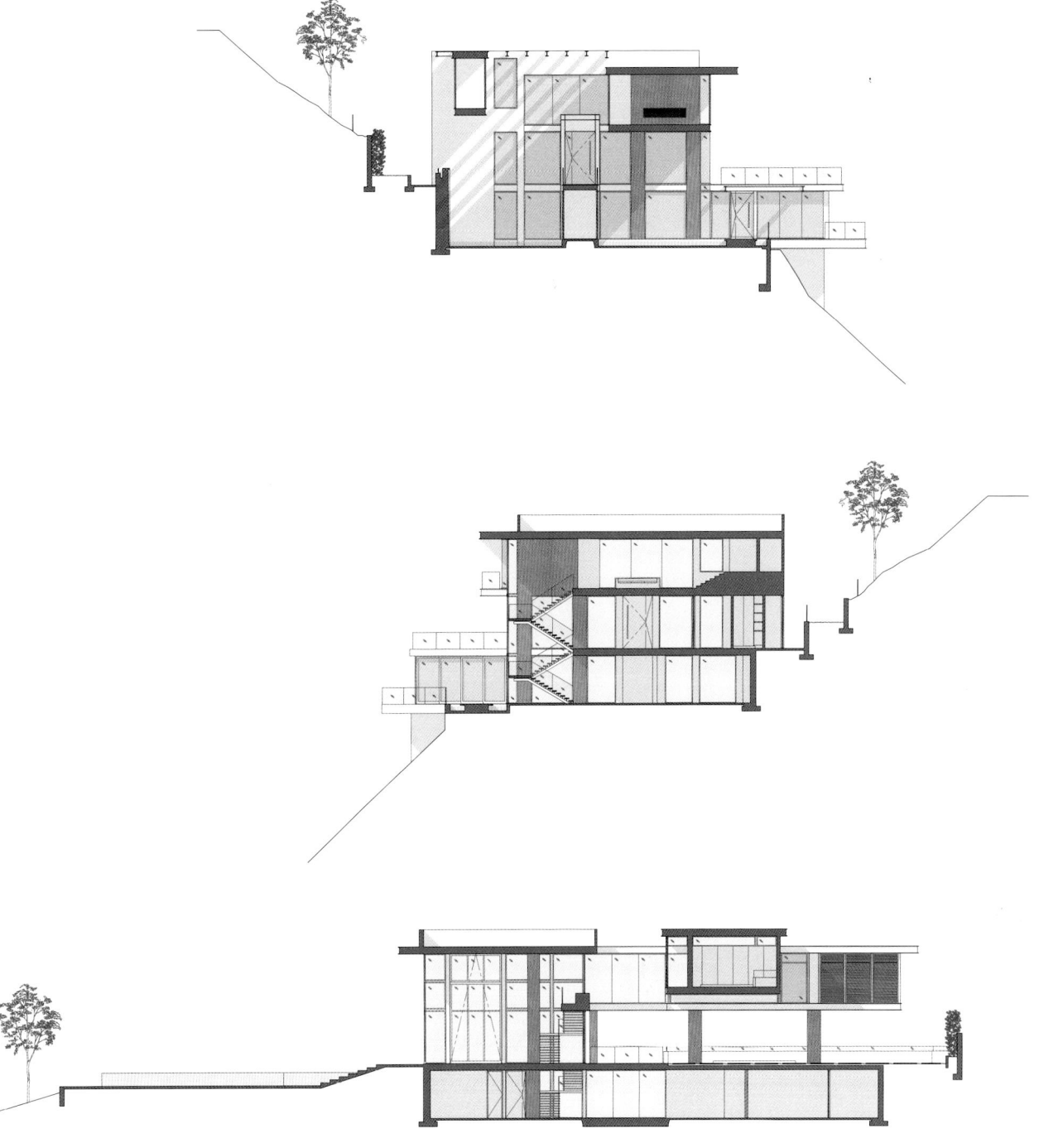

SECTIONS

APPENDIX

Canyon Acres
Completion Date: 2002
Owner: Patty Sieveke
Contractor: Patty Sieveke
Structural Engineer: Structures, Inc
Photographer: Sven Etzelberger

Temple Hills
Completion Date: 2003
Owner: Bonnie Glover
Contractor: Ken McMurray Construction
Structural Engineer: Structures, Inc.
Photographer: Sven Etzelberger

Gainsborough
Completion Date: 2005
Owner: Maria & Lucas Hekma
Contractor: Lucas Hekma
Structural Engineer: Structures, Inc.
Photographer: Sven Etzelberger

Point Place
Completion Date: 2005
Owner: Jeff Thomas
Contractor: John Harwood/Gallo Builders
Structural Engineer: Structures, Inc.
Photographer: Sven Etzelberger

Monarch Bay
Completion Date: 2006
Owner: Monica & Scott Duggan
Contractor: John Harwood
Structural Engineer: Structures, Inc.

Victoria
Completion Date: 2006
Owner: Patrick & Maura McKillen
Contractor: Dan McKeown Construction
Structural Engineer: Robert Lawson Structural Engineers
Photographer: Sven Etzelberger

Alta Laguna
Completion Date: 2007
Owner: Kevin & Michelle Struss
Contractor: Gallo Builders
Structural Engineer: Structures, Inc.
Photographer: Sven Etzelberger

Eagle Rock
Completion Date: 2007
Owner: Katie Lang
Contractor: John Harwood
Structural Engineer: Structures, Inc.
Photographer: Sven Etzelberger

St. Ann's
Completion Date: 2007
Owner: Jeff LaPour
Contractor: Gallo Corporation
Structural Engineer: Structures, Inc.
Interior Designer: Krista Schaeffer

Beach Road
Completion Date: 2008
Owner: Stuart Flamm
Contractor: Gallo Builders
Structural Engineer: Structures, Inc.
Interior Designer: Jill Susson
Photographer: Sven Etzelberger

page 32

Blue Jay Way
Completion Date: 2008
Owner: Brad Kuish
Contractor: Corr Contemporary Homes
Structural Engineer: Lawson-Burke
Interior Designer: Ryan Brown
Photographer: Nick Springett

Mindelheim
Completion Date: 2008
Owner: Tobias Waltl
Contractor: Wagner Moebel
Structural Engineer: Martin Huber Dipl Ing
Interior Designer: Wagner Moebel
Photographer: Paul McClean

page 24

Via Majorca
Completion Date: 2008
Owner: Joan & Eric Davidson
Contractor: Gallo Builders
Structural Engineer: Structures, Inc.
Interior Designer: Joan Davidson
Photographer: Jim Bartsch

Panorama
Completion Date: 2009
Owner: Jeff Day
Contractor: Tom Wessberg
Structural Engineer: EDI/FME, Inc.
Photographer: Sven Etzelberger

Tanager
Completion Date: 2010
Owner: Nile Niami
Contractor: Nile Niami
Structural Engineer: Greg Riley
Interior Designer: Nile Niami
Photographer: Nick Springett

Beverly Hills
Completion Date: 2011
Owner: Nile Niami/McKillen Development
Contractor: Nile Niami/McKillen Development
Structural Engineer: Greg Riley
Interior Designer: Nile Niami/McKillen Development
Photographer: Nick Springett & Sven Etzelberger

page 44

Sarbonne
Completion Date: 2011
Owner: Nile Niami
Contractor: Nile Niami
Structural Engineer: Greg Riley
Photographer: Jim Bartsch & Nick Springett

Washington
Completion Date: 2011
Owner: Coalition Media Group LLC
Contractor: Craig Williams
Structural Engineer: MJM Engineering
Photographer: Luke Gibson

page 54

Oriole Drive
Completion Date: 2012
Owner: Nile Niami/McKillen Development
Contractor: Nile Niami/McKillen Development
Structural Engineer: Greg Riley
Interior Designer: Nile Niami/McKillen Development
Photographer: Jim Bartsch

page 64

Oriole Way
Completion Date: 2012
Owner: Nile Niami
Contractor: Nile Niami
Structural Engineer: Greg Riley
Interior Designer: Nile Niami
Photographer: Jim Bartsch

Tanager II
Completion Date: 2012
Owner: Nile Niami
Contractor: Nile Niami
Structural Engineer: Greg Riley
Interior Designer: Nile Niami
Photographer: Jim Bartsch

Hazel
Completion Date: 2013
Owner: Stephen Beaumont
Contractor: Finton Construction
Structural Engineer: Structures, Inc.

page 74

San Vicente
Completion Date: 2013
Owner: Ralph & Gila Massey
Contractor: Corr Contemporary Homes
Structural Engineer: Structures, Inc.
Photographer: Jim Bartsch

Seacliff
Completion Date: 2013
Owner: McKillen Development
Contractor: Corr Contemporary Homes
Structural Engineer: Structures, Inc.
Photographer: Nick Springett

Beverly Hills II
Completion Date: 2014
Owner: Jasmin Invesment Partners, LLC
Contractor: Tyler Development
Structural Engineer: Structures, Inc.
Interior Designer: Antonia Hutt
Photographer: Jim Bartsch

Blue Jay Way II
Completion Date: 2014
Owner: Dr. Eric & Lily Fugier
Structural Engineer: Structures, Inc.

page 86

Carla Ridge
Completion Date: 2014
Owner: Nile Niami
Contractor: Hamilton Brothers
Structural Engineer: Parker-Resnick
Interior Designer: Nile Niami
Photographer: Jim Bartsch

Stradella
Completion Date: 2014
Owner: Joseph Englanoff
Contractor: Travis Roderick
Structural Engineer: Parker-Resnick
Photographer: Simon Berlyn

page 104

Tanager III
Completion Date: 2014
Owner: McKillen Development
Contractor: McKillen Development
Structural Engineer: Structures, Inc.
Interior Designer: McKillen Development
Photographer: Jim Bartsch &
Nick Springett

page 96

Temple Hills
Completion Date: 2014
Owner: Johanna & Michael Ellis
Contractor: Gallo Builders
Structural Engineer: Structures, Inc.
Interior Designer: Kristin Nugent
Photographer: Jim Bartsch

Sirrine
Completion Date: 2015
Contractor: Gallo Builders
Structural Engineer: Structures, Inc.
Interior Designer: Saskia McClean
Photographer: Jim Bartsch

Vallejo
Completion Date: 2015
Owner: Tara & Bryan Meehan
Contractor: Nova Design Builds
Structural Engineer: Santos-Surrutia
Interior Designer: Tara Meehan

page 112

Williams
Completion Date: 2015
Owner: Nile Niami
Contractor: Hamilton Brothers
Structural Engineer: Parker-Resnick
Interior Designer: Nile Niami/Katie Rotondi
Photographer: Jim Bartsch

Casale
Completion Date: 2016
Owner: Rex Licklider
Contractor: Tyler Development
Structural Engineer: KNA Engineering
Interior Designer: Lynda Murray
Photographer: Jim Bartsch

page 120

Doheny
Completion Date: 2016
Owner: Cody Leibel & James Curnin
Contractor: Craig Williams
Structural Engineer: Structures, Inc.
Interior Designer: Lynda Murray
Photographer: Jim Bartsch

page 128

Hillcrest
Completion Date: 2016
Owner: Perry & Joseph Elihu
Contractor: Perry Elihu
Structural Engineer: Habib Solemani
Interior Designer: Joseph Elihu
Photographer: Jim Bartsch

page 138

Marcheeta
Completion Date: 2016
Owner: Cody Leibel & James Curnin
Contractor: Craig Williams
Structural Engineer: Structures, Inc.
Interior Designer: Lynda Murray
Photographer: Jim Bartsch

page 148

Hillcrest II
Completion Date: 2016
Owner: Nile Niami
Contractor: Hamilton Brothers
Structural Engineer: Parker-Resnick
Interior Designer: Nile Niami/ Katie Rotondi
Photographer: Jim Bartsch/ Simon Berlyn

page 158

Blue Jay Way (remodel)
Completion Date: 2017
Owner: Tim Bergling
Contractor: Gallo Builders
Structural Engineer: Lawson-Burke
Interior Designer: Lynda Murray
Photographer: Simon Berlyn

page 158

Blue Jay Way III
Completion Date: 2017
Owner: Cody Leibel & Leor Yerushalmi
Contractor: Craig Williams
Structural Engineer: John Labib
Interior Designer: Lynda Murray
Photographer: Jim Bartsch

Cuesta
Completion Date: 2017
Owner: McKillen Development
Contractor: McKillen Development
Structural Engineer: John Labib
Interior Designer: McKillen Development
Photographer: Jim Bartsch

page 168

Devlin
Completion Date: 2017
Owner: McKillen Development
Contractor: McKillen Development
Structural Engineer: John Labib
Interior Designer: McKillen Development
Photographer: Jim Bartsch/Simon Berlyn

page 202

Bel Air
Completion Date: 2018
Owner: Raj Kanodia
Contractor: Tyler Development
Structural Engineer: John Labib
Interior Designer: Lynda Murray
Photographer: Simon Berlyn

page 214

Carla Lane
Completion Date: 2018
Owner: Lindsay Chambers
Contractor: Craig Williams
Structural Engineer: Parker-Resnick
Interior Designer: Lindsay Chambers
Photographer: Jim Bartsch

Londonderry
Completion Date: 2018
Owner: Nile Niami
Contractor: Nile Niami
Structural Engineer: Parker-Resnick
Interior Designer: Nile Niami/Katie Rotondi
Photographer: Jim Bartsch

page 180

Robin
Completion Date: 2018
Owner: Francesco Aquilini
Contractor: JD Group
Structural Engineer: Parker-Resnick
Photographer: Simon Berlyn

page 192

Sunridge
Completion Date: 2018
Owner: Francesco Aquilini
Contractor: Vision Pacific
Photographer: Ema Peter

page 224

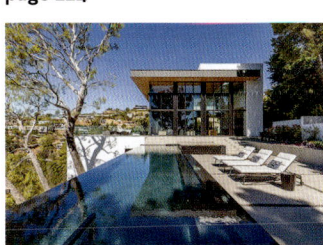

Skylark
Completion Date: 2018
Owner: Jason Rubin
Contractor: Gallo Builders
Structural Engineer: Parker-Resnick
Interior Designer: Michael Fullen
Photographer: Jim Bartsch

First published in the United States of America in 2019 by
Rizzoli International Publications, Inc.
300 Park Avenue South
New York, NY 10010
www.rizzoliusa.com

Designed by Claudia Brandenburg

Rizzoli Editor: Ellen R. Cohen

ISBN: 978-0-8478-6350-1
Library of Congress Control Number: 2018964212

Copyright © 2019 Paul McClean

All rights reserved. No part of this publication may be reproduced,
stored in a retrieval system, or transmitted in any form or by any
means, electronic, mechanical, photocopying, recording, or otherwise,
without prior consent of the publisher.

Printed in Hong Kong

2022 2023 2024 2025 / 10 9 8 7 6 5 4